MW00523175

MATCHED

4MARRIAGE

MEANT 4LIFE

MATCHED
4MARRIAGE
MEANT 4LIFE

Solving the Mystery
of Relationships

NATE STEVENS

TATE PUBLISHING & Enterprises

Published by Tate Publishing & Enterprises, LLC
127 E. Trade Center Terrace | Mustang, Oklahoma 73064 USA
1.888.361.9473 | www.tatepublishing.com

Tate Publishing is committed to excellence in the publishing industry. The company reflects the philosophy established by the founders, based on Psalm 68:11,
"The Lord gave the word and great was the company of those who published it."

Book design copyright © 2011 by Tate Publishing, LLC. All rights reserved.
Cover design by Kris Swiatocho and Leah LeFlore
Interior design by Nate Stevens and Leah LeFlore

Published in the United States of America

ISBN: 978-1-61346-295-9
1. Love & Marriage, Christian Life, Religion
2. Family & Relationships, Marriage
11.04.02

*Don't look for someone perfect—
look for the one who is perfect for you.*

Dedication

To my two dear children, Melissa and Mitchell, who are uniquely different, yet wonderfully and marvelously special—and much better than I deserve.

You are growing up far too quickly; but like every parent knows, I can do nothing to slow the passage of time. I can only do my very best to prepare you for life by giving you the relational instruction I wish I had received when I was your age. By drawing on my own life experiences (both good and bad), the life experiences of others as related to my research, and the wisdom found in God's Word, I offer you this with the sincere hope and earnest prayer that it encourages you in your relational pursuit to find your life-long compatible spouses.

As you grow and develop into the adults God intends for you to become, please keep one important thing in mind—never settle for less than full relational interdependence and complete compatibility in all four aspects of life.

I love you both with all that I am!

Foreword

Dear Daddy,

Thank you so much for telling me every time I saw you about the importance of finding "the right one." I can see us now, riding in the car up to your house for the weekend, and you going over "one more time" about the four aspects of compatibility. I'm very glad you wrote your insights and knowledge about the four aspects of relationships and love into this book—not only for me, but for everyone. I hope that everyone who reads this will find that special someone with whom they are perfectly compatible for the rest of their lifetime. It is never too late for anyone to find that last puzzle piece. I will always remember all the wonderful analogies you used—especially the puzzle. I will never ever forget how much you love me and care for me. It is nice knowing that you care enough to want me to be happy for the rest of my life. I love you so much, daddy!

Yours (until I find "him") Forever,

Melissa

Prologue

If there has ever been a needed piece of literary work, it is this book. *Matched 4 Marriage—Meant 4 Life* is a subject that should concern every person who has ever contemplated marriage. The four aspects of relational pursuits, with which the author deals, are an essential part of any husband-wife relationship. Both people should carefully consider these four aspects long before a ring goes on the finger of the bride to be.

Sadly, most weddings today take place without proper discovery by both parties regarding the elements required for a happy, long-term experience. I have performed literally hundreds of weddings during my forty-six and one half year ministry as a pastor. Usually when a prospective bride would call, I would require her and her fiancée to set up an appointment together so I could talk to them both at the same time. Very often, even finding a time to get them together before the wedding was difficult not to mention the idea of giving them any counsel. During the appointment, which rarely lasted more than one hour, most of the time was spent planning the details of the wedding. This would leave perhaps fifteen minutes or less for marital counseling about the lifelong journey they were about to start. I have long since retired from the pastorate; but how I wish that this book had been available years ago. I would have made it mandatory reading for all couples contemplating marriage.

I have known Nate Stevens for over twenty years. I have been his pastor as well as an uncle by marriage. He served under my ministry as a brilliant Sunday School teacher and as a member of the church's finance committee. We have not always seen eye to eye, but I have always held deep respect for his academic and spiritual insight. He has been very successful in business and his academic pursuits. He earned a Bachelors Degree as well as an MBA. We have talked together, prayed together and even discussed Greek together (Nate having read / studied the New Testament in Greek, a feat far beyond my very limited knowledge of the language). I am well old enough to be his father. A time or two, I have even felt he needed to be taken to the woodshed. That not withstanding, he has written a very much-needed book. He has done a masterful job analyzing long-term relationships and presenting them in an understandable and interesting manner. I suggest that you read patiently and carefully what he has to say. It could well save you much misery in the future as well as enable you to avoid some in the present by applying what he has written.

Pleasant reading,

Dr. Jack J. Dinsbeer
Pastor Emeritus University Baptist Church
Jacksonville, Florida

Table of Contents

Preface

Relationship issues affect every one of us in one way or another. Even if you are in a satisfying relationship, you probably know someone who is not. A quick online search confirms that divorce affects anywhere from a third to nearly half of all marriages. Committed relationships and marriage have become hurried and experimental. Or they are avoided at all costs. Rarely are they strategically planned and enjoyed for a lifetime. There are examples all around us of relationships that are unhappy, unfulfilled, mediocre, strained, or confrontational. How many marriages can you point to and say, "That's the kind of marriage I want"? Yes, they do exist. But they are far too few.

I wish I had learned this book's lessons much earlier in life. When I was young and single, I dreamed of having a picture-perfect marriage. Even though I "followed all the rules" I knew at the time, my marriage still ended in divorce. Those "rules" included having a daily quiet time of Bible study and prayer, looking for a spouse who was a Christian, regularly attending and being involved in church ministry, and staying sexually pure until marriage. I thought if I found an attractive Christian woman, felt passionately "in love" about her, and shared a similar life purpose with her, God would miraculously bless us with a happy, fulfilling, and ecstatic marriage.

In looking back, I now realize how naïve and wrong that presumption was. I was not even close to being ready for marriage. Even though I found spiritual and intellectual common ground with my partner prior to marriage, I gave no serious thought to emotional or physical compatibility. I assumed that if I found spiritual common ground and felt those "love butterflies" inside, somehow the emotional connection, physical desire, and sexual expectations would all fall into place. My immaturity, lack of preparation, foolish choices, and avoidable mistakes resulted in heartache and a broken family.

From that marriage, God blessed me with two incredible children whom I love dearly. Since they are now teenagers and facing the "dating years," I want to give them some meaningful and basic instruction about successful relationships that I did not have when I was their age. I wish to better prepare my kids to make wiser choices than I did. And hopefully help them avoid similar problems and pain. I hope the same for you as well.

This book is not about the "Five Easy Steps to Finding a Mate." Nor is it Cupid's handbook on how to make someone fall in love with you. It is not filled with unrealistic romance-novel expectations. It is also not the work of a licensed counselor, minister, psychologist, psychiatrist, or theologian. Instead, it is the wise counsel of a loving father who learned these lessons the hard way.

Matched 4 Marriage—Meant 4 Life describes the four aspects of life—spiritual, intellectual, emotional, and physical. It explains the importance of fully developing the spirit, mind, soul, and body; then it shows how each aspect should influence the search for a spouse. It encourages an *interdependent* relationship as the healthy alternative to *dependence* or *independence*. Also identified are the enduring behaviors involved in a lasting and enjoyable marriage. My goal for this book is to lead the reader to a balanced, abundant life and a rewarding journey toward a compatible, fulfilling, and lifelong marriage.

The target audience for this book is single adults—those who have never been married or are single again—and anyone related to or associated with a single adult. Instead of a *reactive* effort to repair troubled marriages, I encourage the "unmarrieds" with a *proactive* approach of "Let's do it right the first time." Hopefully,

> Instead of a *reactive* effort to repair troubled marriages, take a *proactive* approach of "Let's do it right the first time."

this book will challenge existing mindsets and help restore the enjoyment, fulfillment, and permanence of marriage that God intends. *It is attainable!*

To the single young adults and those who are single again: slow down in your hurry to find a spouse. Control your strong desire for intimate companionship. Take the time to fully develop all four aspects of your life. Discover and pursue relational *interdependence*. Never settle for less than complete compatibility in all four aspects. Learn from the mistakes others have made in their relationships. Then do everything possible to avoid similar mistakes in your life.

To the parents of teenagers and single young adults: share the principles in this book with your children. Equip them to pursue the satisfaction, enjoyment, and fulfillment of a healthy relationship. These are not merely dreams in the fantasy world of movies or romance novels. They are definite realities God intends for marriage.

Ministers, Bible study teachers, and counselors: incorporate this book's message into your sermons and presentations. Use it as a starting point for group study and discussion. Instead of focusing solely on the *spiritual* aspect, inspire people to develop healthy completion in *all four* aspects.

Youth pastors and guidance counselors: introduce young adults to the incredible relationship possibilities God has in store for those who follow His plan. Encourage them to develop themselves fully and to seek compatibility in all four aspects *before* becoming emotionally attached or involved in a committed relationship. Emphasize that God expects us to fully experience, express, and enjoy life in spirit, mind, soul, and body. But caution them to follow the proper relational progression and timing to gain God's blessing.

High school teachers and college professors: integrate this theme in your classroom and lectures, even in institutions that are not faith-based. Challenge your students to succeed not only in their future careers, but also in their future homes.

To all my readers, may you find true relationship compatibility and fulfillment by applying these insights on your journey to finding "the one" with whom you are *Matched 4 Marriage and Meant 4 Life.*

THE MYSTERY OF RELATIONSHIPS

There are three things that are too amazing for me,
four that I do not understand:
the way of an eagle in the sky,
the way of a snake on a rock,
the way of a ship on the high seas,
and the way of a man with a maiden.
(Proverbs 30:18-19)

Introduction

When Proverbs 30:18-19 was written, the laws of aerodynamics, reptile locomotion, and sailing would not have been thoroughly understood. However, many scientific discoveries over the centuries have solved the first three mysteries.

Yet, as much as we've learned over the years, the fourth mystery remains: the way of a man with a woman. Many relationship books and articles unlock various parts of it. But the mystery remains. Romantic relationships are still confusing and challenging.

Many of us initially approach relationships with little strategy or forethought. We simply move through life within our established social circles and make our relational choices based on whatever criteria we believe is important at the time.

> Many of us initially approach relationships with little strategy or forethought.

If someone is available, attractive, humorous, upbeat, and financially stable, we feel safe to pursue a relationship with that person.

We may listen to various authority figures in our lives when they share their "realistic" perspectives on marriage. They tell us, *Marriage isn't all it's cracked up to be. Marriage is about hard work, sac-*

rifice, and giving in. There is no perfect person or perfect marriage. Reality hits when the honeymoon is over. Now doesn't that make marriage sound like fun?

As a result of this "constructive" guidance, instead of approaching marriage with confidence and celebration, we approach it with a sense of hope and apprehension. Some people go so far as to create prenuptial agreements to plan for what happens *when* their marriage fails.

Sometimes we base our relationship choices on our impulsive feelings, rushing down the aisle because of our sense of giddy pleasure or uncontrolled hormones. We may become impatient, so we "settle" for a less-than-ideal choice so we can "get on with life." Or we give in to pressure from friends and family members who believe there must be something wrong with us if we aren't married by a certain age. We may even find ourselves in a situation where, due to previous promiscuous and immoral choices, we believe we should "do the right thing" and get married. Basically, we choose as best we can, then hope for the best.

But what if it were possible to solve the mystery of relationships in a way that involved less hope and more strategy? Less depressing guidance and more inspirational instruction? Fewer painful results and more fulfillment and enjoyment? Are you interested? If so, are you ready to prepare yourself to have the happy, meaningful, and fulfilling marriage God intends for you? Then read on!

CHAPTER 1

It's a Mystery

Our experience with love is confusing and everyone has an opinion. Pastoral pre-marital counseling can lead you on the right track.

> *Love is patient, love is kind.*
> *It does not envy, it does not boast, it is not proud.*
> *It is not rude, it is not self-seeking, it is not easily*
> *angered, it keeps no record of wrongs.*
> *Love does not delight in evil but rejoices with the truth.*
> *It always protects, always trusts, always hopes, always perseveres.*
> *Love never fails.*
> *(I Corinthians 13:4-8)*

Do you remember what it felt like the first time you fell head-over-heels in love? The person of your dreams paid you a compliment, smiled in your direction, or wished you a happy day. Your heart fluttered. Your mind raced. Your soul melted. Your body tingled. You felt lightheaded. Your palms got sweaty. Your temperature started rising. You felt certain this was "love at first sight." Never mind that all those symptoms could mean you have the flu!

> Do you remember what it felt like the first time you fell head-over-heels in love?

There was an extra zing in your step. Sweet "love music" was ringing in your ears. There was a feeling of belonging in your heart; a new realization that the world was not such a bad place after all. You wore a perpetual smile on your face. You daydreamed of the places you would see and the things you would do together. You firmly believed you found "the one," the person meant exclusively for you.

This person understood you. Accepted you. Said all the right things to make you feel wonderful. Brought a bit of sunshine to your ordinary or dreary life. Just rubbing elbows or touching pinky fingers electrified you. You couldn't wait until the next time you saw or spoke to each other. You considered yourself the luckiest person in the world. Maybe even the universe!

Then the bottom fell out.

You found out this wonderful person did not feel the same way you did. The "love music" you heard was not mutually shared. Other people, places, things, and interests were more important than a deep, meaningful relationship with you.

Maybe circumstances changed. Perhaps both of you did not simultaneously arrive at the same intersection of life. Maybe you enjoyed a close relationship for a while, yet the fateful day came when you knew it was over. You heard those dreaded words, "Let's just be friends." Or you received the heartless text message that merely said, "C ya."

You were devastated. Heartbroken. Torn completely apart inside. Dazed and dumbfounded, you asked, "What went wrong? How could something that felt so right turn out so horribly? Where did the 'magic' go? What happened to all the incredible dreams and plans we had for the future?"

Sound familiar? Welcome to the "mystery" of relationships.

With the passing of time, we think we've learned from our experiences. However, with each new heartbreak the mystery gets more complicated. We begin to wonder if there are any favorable answers to our longing for true companionship.

> *Every instance of heartbreak can teach us powerful lessons about creating the kind of love we really want. The only way to graduate from Heartbreak Academy is to really master the material, and that means absorbing crucial lessons about your true self, your true needs, and the nature of true love.*[1]

In our quest to solve this mystery, we turn to many sources. Numerous Web sites, books, and women's magazines offer relationship advice, testimonials, and surveys on how to find "Mr. Right." Many provide questionnaires promising to help you identify the characteristics of "the one," including height, physique, type of vehicle he drives, number of tattoos, etc. Then there's his career choice, salary, and the size of his financial portfolio.

Once you find this "perfect mate," these "experts" tell you what questions you should ask, what signs to look for, and how to treat him. Some even offer advice on tantalizing sexual techniques that are guaranteed to capture his attention.

Men's magazines offer similar advice on how to know if a woman is "the right one." They give dating tips that include clues on reading body language, how to act interested in a woman by listening attentively (even if he is not truly interested in the topic), how to flirt effectively, and other mind games.

There are lists of requirements that include her appearance, hairstyle, clothing fashions, and amount of cosmetics required. How she fills out a pair of jeans, how well endowed she is, and specific body measurements. There's also advice on how to tell if she's a "gold digger" (more interested in your checkbook than in you). The "experts" give advice and rating systems on styles, types, and preferences of kissing. They even encourage trying the latest "seduction moves" to speed up the trip to the bedroom.

Young adults and singles listen to all this advice in their attempt to avoid the heartache associated with being lonely. They want to love and be loved by someone special. They want to be accepted by and connected with someone. Unfortunately, their desires often lead to making foolish and impulsive choices that result in rejection, negative consequences, and heartache.

Very few young adults and singles seek their parents' advice on finding the right mate. When it comes to relationship guidance, parents don't seem approachable. They're "so not cool" or "with it." *Besides, what do parents know about true love?*

> The relationship behavior children see modeled by their parents is often repeated in their own lives.

Many parents are uncomfortable talking about this subject with their kids. Maybe because their parents did not discuss it with them. Mom and Dad may be struggling with their own relationship "mystery" and have no substantial advice to give. Some young adults may observe the unemotional, detached, obligatory, or confrontational relationships their parents have and do not want to follow their example. And yet, the relationship behavior children see modeled by their parents is often repeated in their own lives. Then the cycle of incompatible behavior continues.[2]

Even churches, schools, and public-service organizations can be confusing and disappointing in their effort to provide relationship guidance. Their lists of "do's" and "don'ts" seem rather illogical. Some groups offer sex education that promotes sexual activity as acceptable for teens as long as they use "protection." The Sexuality Information and Education Council of the United States (SIECUS) developed guidelines for sex education that have become "one of the most influential publications in the field."

These guidelines call for teaching five- through eight-year-olds about masturbation, sexual intercourse, accept-

In the multitude of Counselors . . .

ing cohabitation, and homosexuality. Upper elementary students learn about these topics as well as contraception and abortion. Topics for junior high students include sexual fantasies, body massages, and oral, vaginal, and anal intercourse. For high school students, SIECUS recommends adding discussion about using "erotic photographs" [otherwise known as pornography] and literature. Only one page out of one hundred is dedicated to abstinence.[3]

At the other end of the spectrum, religious groups spew fire and brimstone about the sensual depravity and carnal sinfulness of sex while ignoring its importance and downplaying its pleasure— sometimes even after marriage!

Dr. James Dobson, founder and Chairman Emeritus of Focus on the Family, offers this insight on the devastating effects these misguided attitudes can have on people, their perceptions, and their future relationships:

Adult attitudes toward sexual relations are a function of genetics and conditioning during childhood and adolescence. It is surprising to observe how many otherwise well-adjusted people still think of married sex as dirty, animalistic, or evil. Such a person who has been taught a one-sided, negative approach to sex during the formative years may find it impossible to release these carefully constructed inhibitions on the wedding night. The marriage ceremony is simply insufficient to reorient one's attitude from "Thou shalt not" to "Thou shalt—regularly—and with great passion!" That mental turnabout is not easily achieved.[4]

Both perspectives—the unrestrained, immoral encouragement and the "religious" guilt trips—unwittingly add more confusion to the relational mystery and contribute to strained or failed relationships.

Though the trend appears headed for disaster, bright spots of hope exist. Some churches and organizations include "premarital mentoring" in their counseling efforts:

> *Real premarital preparation doesn't mean spending an hour or two with a pastor planning a wedding ceremony. Premarital mentoring is much more. It involves helping couples dig deep to understand needs, expectations, differences, communication, conflict resolution, finances, sex, in-laws, and more. It involves assessing their readiness for marriage and determining their compatibility. Sometimes it means they discover they are neither ready nor compatible—and that's okay.*[5]

Premarital mentoring encourages couples to get to know each other apart from their feelings. They learn about marital interaction from the experiences of married couples. Unmarried couples are given a chance to visualize how marriage might look for them. This kind of mentoring either strengthens the relationship or reveals incompatibilities that should be talked about while still dating. If these differences cannot be resolved, the dating couple becomes aware that their relationship should not lead to marriage.

Even with all the advice that bombards us today, the relational mystery can still seem confusing and complicated. Perhaps it is too difficult, time consuming, and overwhelming to ever understand. So we give up. We give in to our strong feelings for someone or we impatiently "settle" for whoever comes closest to our requirements or standards. Then we deal with the resulting emptiness as best we can.

But life doesn't *have* to be this way. There is hope! The mystery can be solved! God wants every person to live an abundant life—and He gives us the clues to achieve it. Not just spiritually, but intellectually, emotionally, and physically as well. Not just for an abundant life personally, but also in your marriage.

CHAPTER 2

We Need Help Solving the Mystery

[handwritten annotations: "and look at the statistics)" above title; "We have a mess. The world's input is usually detrimental and the ___" below title]

few people do manage to find their "true love." Their "one and only." They laugh together. Flirt with each other. Enjoy each other's company. Share a mutual connection that makes everyone around them disgusted or jealous. Even their disagreements seem like fun! But for most people, a happy and fulfilling relationship exists only in their dreams. "Mr. Right" simply doesn't exist. "Mrs. Right" is just an idealistic fantasy. If they really do exist, finding them must be random luck.

To make matters worse, we face pressure every day to give in to short-term pleasure at the expense of long-term satisfaction. Magazines, movies, television programs, commercials, even computer games encourage us to live without moral restraint. Invitations to instant gratification and pleasure tempt us in every area of our lives. *[handwritten annotation: "Redeem the time"]*

Two major influencers of our society, Hollywood and prime-time television, only make the problem worse. Movies and TV programs portray sex in the context of marriage as either nonexistent or too restrictive. Extramarital sexual relationships are presented as normal. Verbal references to sex outside of marriage outnumber references to marital sex by nearly three to one. Scenes showing or implying sex between unmarried partners outnumber similar scenes between married couples by nearly four to one.[6]

> *Children and teens are now exposed to a host of sexual behaviors that less than a generation ago would have been considered off-limits for broadcast television. Some of the once-taboo-for-TV sexual behaviors that are now found on prime time television include threesomes, partner swapping, pedophilia, necrophilia, bestiality, and sex with prostitutes, in addition to depictions of strippers, references to masturbation, pornography, sex toys, and kinky or fetishistic behaviors. Behaviors that were once seen as fringe, immoral, or socially destructive have been given the stamp of approval by the television industry. And recent studies show that children are influenced by those messages.[7]*

Young adults grow up in the midst of this moral assault. It desensitizes them. They are influenced not only to accept immoral lifestyles but also to casually experiment with them. When they do look for guidance and direction, the people who seem to have the real answers are silenced under the pressure of four dangerous concepts:

- *Political correctness* that promotes a universal fear of offending anyone
- *Unchecked tolerance* that endorses all views, no matter their validity
- *Blind acceptance* of perceived truth that clouds people's minds to absolute truth
- *Religious legalism* that manipulates biblical teaching to support a particular denomination, personal preference, or chosen lifestyle

In the face of the immoral pressure from the world and the absence of sound relationship guidance, young adults and singles are left

Marry Later

to figure it out on their own. Unfortunately, many make avoidable mistakes. Marriages take place for many illogical reasons. Uncontrolled sexual desires. An unexpected pregnancy. Desired social status. Parental expectations. Peer pressure. Loneliness. Young couples think their good intentions will reward them with wedded bliss. And some do find it. But many do not.

Although we all tend to believe that nothing bad will ever happen to us, our unwise and immoral choices contribute to these stunning negative statistics involving divorce, the family breakdown, premarital sex, sexual diseases, and marital unhappiness.

Divorce

- Approximately fifty percent of first marriages end in divorce.[8] Those who make poor choices in relationships usually end up living with the heartache of divorce or an unhappy marriage.
- To avoid the pain and hassle of divorce, more people are choosing just to live together. The percentage of people getting married is steadily dropping (59 percent). The percentage of unmarried couples living together that are male-female unions is an alarming 89 percent.[9] This arrangement directly opposes God's plan for marriage.
- Sixty percent of remarriages fail. And they fail much quicker than first marriages. After an average of ten years, 37 percent of remarriages fail versus 30 percent of first marriages.[10] This confirms that divorce does not necessarily resolve the problems experienced in the previous marriage. Some "issues" we carry with us.

Family Breakdown

- Along with divorce comes the breakup of the family and associated negative consequences. Fatherless homes account for 63 percent of youth suicides, 90 percent of homeless or runaway children, 85 percent of children with behavior problems,

71 percent of high school dropouts, 85 percent of youths in prison, and well over 50 percent of unwed teen mothers.[11]

Premarital Sex

- In the absence of godly premarital counsel and moral restraint, teenagers casually experiment with sex. In 2003, 62 percent of twelfth graders indicated they had sexual intercourse.[12]
- In 2006, nearly half (46%) of all fifteen-to-nineteen-year-olds in the United States have had sex at least once.[13] Teenagers who have barely learned how to drive a car are carelessly engaging in the most intimate and life-changing act.
- Ten percent of young women aged eighteen to twenty-four who had sex before age twenty report that their first sexual experience was *involuntary*.[14] For the rest of their lives, they will carry the memory of that violent and harsh encounter.
- About one third of ninth- to twelfth-grade women become pregnant at least once before they reach the age of twenty.[15] That is about 820,000 teenage mothers each year!
- In 2006, 27 percent of pregnancies among fifteen- to nineteen-year-olds ended with abortions. The reasons that are most frequently given by teenage mothers for abortion include concern about how having a baby would change their lives, inability to afford a baby, and feeling insufficiently mature to raise a child.[18]

Sexual Diseases

- Each year, there are 9.1 million new cases of sexually transmitted infections among fifteen- to twenty-four-year olds.[16] This should motivate every unmarried person to stay sexually pure until marriage!
- More than 65 million people in the United States have an incurable sexually transmitted disease. In 1998, nearly 30,000 people died in the US from an STD or its effects.[17]

Marital Unhappiness

- For those couples who choose to stay married, almost half are unhappy with their marriage. In a recent survey, only 54 percent of participants rated their marital happiness as an eight or higher (on a scale of zero to ten where zero means very unhappy and ten means very happy).[19]

Aside from the effects on individuals and families, these poor relationship choices are also quite expensive. The costly consequences of sustained divorce rates and childbearing outside of marriage include an annual cost to US taxpayers of $112 billion—more than $1 trillion each decade.[20] These costs involve medical expenses associated with abortions, educational programs, anti-poverty benefits, and criminal justice system expense.

All these heartbreaking facts, statistics, and information confirm one glaring truth. We *must* solve the mystery of relationships. For our own sake. For our children's sake. For our nation's sake. But we need help. *We cannot continue following the present course of action.* We can't keep doing the same things while expecting better results.

> We can't keep doing the same things while expecting better results.

Instead of being envious of the happy couples we encounter, we should figure out what makes their relationships successful. Instead of dreaming about a satisfying relationship, we should find answers from reliable and consistent sources. There is significant value in learning from the experiences of others (both successes and failures), in listening to common sense, and in discovering the wisdom found in the Bible.

CHAPTER 3

God's Relationship Clues

The Bible has an answers for what our society preaches

Why should we include the Bible in our search for answers to the relational mystery? Isn't it outdated, prudish, restrictive, and out of touch with today's progressive times and culture? Actually, the Bible is all about relationships. It covers every relational phase. The beginning spark of attraction. Growth and development. Close companionship. Breakups. Reconciliation. Scripture does not sugarcoat relationships, portraying them as some sort of utopian paradise. It reveals their complexity, proper progression, and potential fulfillment—at both divine and human levels.

Here are a few points found in God's Word about relationships:

- The fourth word in Scripture, translated as "God" (Genesis 1:1), is the Hebrew word *Elohim*. It refers to the plurality of the one true God.[21] This plurality identifies God the Father, God the Son, and God the Holy Spirit. The Holy Trinity. This reveals the existence of relationships at a divine level.
- The Old Testament outlines the relationship between God and the people of Israel. His desire for an intimate relationship with them. Their times of closeness and fellowship with

Him. Their repeated rebellion and straying from Him. His judgment and punishment for their disobedient choices. Their subsequent repentance and return to Him. His loving forgiveness and restoration.

- The New Testament reveals God's desire for an intimate relationship with every person. His love for the world. His gift of salvation through Christ's atoning death on the cross. His loving forgiveness and restoration.
- The first four of the Ten Commandments specifically identify our relationship with God (Exodus 20:2-17). The other six commandments involve our human interaction.
- The book of the Song of Solomon is a vivid portrayal of loving interaction between a man and a woman. It describes the affectionate intimacy and physical involvement within a fulfilling and committed marriage.
- Christians are instructed to exhibit love as a sign of their relationship with Christ (John 13:35). This involves loving and compassionate actions within human relationships.
- The final chapter of the last book of the Bible (Revelation 22) describes the return of Christ (as a bridegroom) to be reunited with His followers (the bride). It uses the symbolism of marriage to illustrate that future relationship.

You may ask, *What makes the Bible so special that we should include it as a resource for understanding relationships?* Let's review four main reasons that answer this question.

Logical Approach

Our society has steadily replaced the truth of God's Word with humanistic philosophy and an acceptance of relative truth. *Relativism* is the concept that there is no absolute truth—everyone has his or her own inner sense of truth. "Conceptions of truth and moral values are not absolute but are relative to the persons or groups holding them."[22] As you can imagine, when everyone has his own definition of moral truth and standards, the outcomes will be vastly different and confusing.

We see the foolishness of relativism by using the simple example of a ruler. Imagine if everyone rejected the absolute truth that a foot is equal to twelve inches and replaced it with their individual "sense of truth" and personal preferences of varying number of inches. We would not only be foolish, we would be creating a world of chaos. No matter our personal preferences, absolute truth exists for our benefit.

> When everyone has his own definition of moral truth and standards, the outcomes will be vastly different and confusing.

The effort to replace God's absolute truth with man's relativism has encouraged a rapid decline in cultural and moral values. The result of this decline is seen in the negative relational consequences and the trail of confused and heartbroken people. With the removal of God, His influence, and His moral standard (as found in the Bible) from our daily lives, we are left to figure life out on our own. The discouraging results of our efforts apart from God's help speak for themselves. Logically speaking, it is time to get back to God's Word.

God Invented Relational Intimacy

Contrary to evolutionary theory, God created us. (Anyone needing further clarification of the evolutionary issue should read *The Case for a Creator* by Yale-educated and award-winning author Lee Strobel.)[23] God created the two different genders and invented the institutions of marriage and the family. As our Creator, God knows how we are made. He understands the complexities of both genders. He understands human interaction. He also knows the intimate human relationship He wants us to enjoy.

God invented sex and sexual intimacy. It is His special gift to the human race. As part of His overall creation, He declared it to be "very good" (Genesis 1:31). God intends sex to be fully engaged

> God invented sex and sexual intimacy. As part of His overall creation, He declared it to be very good.

and abundantly enjoyed—but only within the safety and commitment of marriage.

God's Word tells us love is *of* God and God *is* love (I John 4:7-8). Without Him, there is no love. He is the very basis of love. So why not seek relationship answers from the One who invented relational intimacy? We are wise to seek God's guidance on love, sex, and intimacy instead of looking for answers from "relationship experts" who encourage us to casually experiment with sex and cheaply abuse its privileges.

The Test of Time

The Bible stands the test of time as a reliable source of truth. The wisdom and instruction it contains are unchanging and unfailing. God's Word is not affected by our ever changing and downward spiraling moral and cultural standards. We cannot eliminate it, diminish it, or detract from it—but by ignoring it, we only hurt ourselves. It has survived over the years and it will outlast every one of us. "Your word, O Lord, is eternal; it stands firm in the heavens" (Psalm 119:89). "Heaven and earth will pass away, but my words will never pass away" (Luke 21:33). God's Word lasts forever while our brief time on earth passes as quickly as steam vanishes into the air (James 4:14).

The Bible is more reliable than the frequently changing cultural fads where everybody interprets truth as they prefer it or as it fits into their situation. When we try to replace God's Word with whatever source of truth we need to escape from the personal accountability of our choices, we are headed for confusion and disaster. Scripture stands the test of time. Common sense tells us we should pay attention to it and apply it to our lives.

God's Instruction Manual

The Bible is God's instruction manual for His creation. He did not give it to us to lay unopened on the nightstand or coffee table. He meant for us to read it, study it, and apply it to all areas of our lives—including our relationships.

"All Scripture is God-breathed and is useful for teaching, rebuking, correcting and training in righteousness" (II Timothy 3:16). God gave us His Word to provide us a reliable source of information. "The word of God is living and active" (Hebrews 4:12). Scripture is alive; it penetrates our hearts and minds with God's truth. It is described with such trustworthy terms as *perfect, sure, right, and true* (Psalm 19:7-10). God's Word is "flawless" (II Samuel 22:31). No humanistic self-improvement program or dating expert can make such a claim—and back it up.

When we plan a road trip, we consult a map or a GPS. In doing so, we find the most convenient roads, the quickest or shortest routes, or the most scenic drive. This helps us have a safe, enjoyable trip, while ultimately arriving at our desired destination. Similarly, our "road trip" of life contains various directions, decisions, and choices. One of the most significant of these is the choice of a spouse. We can use God's Word as our relationship map for our journey to a compatible, satisfying, and lifelong marriage.

By reviewing God's reliable and unchanging truth, we discover the clues to understanding ourselves and how we can achieve the loving interaction God intends between a husband and wife.

CHAPTER 4

Relational Interaction

Both must be committed & work at it

I*nteraction* is a mutual, two-way action of two individuals.[24] This action or behavior has a shared effect on both people. It combines their effort in their quest and achievement of a common goal. We interact within a relationship while expecting similar action and behavior in return.

Merely being in a relationship does not guarantee loving, two-way interaction. Before getting seriously involved in a relationship, determine your interest and enthusiasm levels as well as your prospective partner's. Successful personal relationships involve give and take. Cause and effect. You scratch my back while I scratch yours. Fulfilling and lasting relationships require mutual (shared) and reciprocal (two-way) levels of importance, intensity, and involvement. If both people are not fully, equally, and exclusively committed, someone will get hurt.

In a one-sided relationship, one person (the *giver*) initiates the affection, tender expression, and attempts at emotional connection while the other person is the clueless or unresponsive

> One-sided relationships generally do not succeed or last for long.

taker. The taker sponges up all the attention, affection, and effort while providing the giver little or nothing in return. Such relationships generally do not succeed or last for long. Usually, givers get frustrated and start looking elsewhere for happiness and fulfillment of their needs. The takers then find new givers who will meet their needs. And the dependent cycle continues.

When love sends its fair messengers
To dance across the stage of your mind
To woo the vulnerabilities of your soul
To test the resolve of your spirit
To enflame the attention of your being
To entangle your heart with the blossom of promise...
Make sure it is real—not based on dependence, infatuation, or surface level adoration
Make sure it is available—not based on some future hopeful turn of events
Make sure it is unconditional—given fully, freely, fiercely, and forever
Make sure it is attentive—no distractions from other priorities
Make sure it is mutual—not simply a one-way dream.
To set your heart on a one-way love is to...
Manufacture dreams on the mirage of wishful thinking
Seek secure footing in the quicksand of anticipation
Build sand castles on the seashore of hope
Grasp firmly to a lifeline of dust.[25]

Our individual complexity, uniqueness, and natural self-centeredness lead us to believe the universe revolves around us. Based on societal values and ambitious pressures, we believe we must "look out for number one." We do this in our personal goals, our career pursuits, and our social circles. We may unintentionally do this in our relationships as well.

This line of thinking stands in direct opposition to biblical values of:

- Holding others in higher regard than ourselves (Philippians 2:3)
- Giving honorable preference to others (Romans 12:10)
- Subordinating our selfish interests to others (Ephesians 5:21; I Peter 5:5)
- Treating others the way we want to be treated (Matthew 7:12)

A self-centered and isolated outlook may sound appealing and protective. However, God does not want us to be self-absorbed or alone. In fact, one of the main reasons He created us was to have ongoing personal interaction (fellowship and companionship) with Him.

> One of the main reasons God created us was to have ongoing personal interaction with Him.

Prior to man's fall into sin, God was in constant contact and communication with Adam and Eve. He would come down in the coolness of the evening just to spend time walking and talking with them in the Garden of Eden (Genesis 3:8).

In addition to being created to have a relationship with God, we were also made to need relational interaction with other people. God didn't create us for unhealthy, one-way, *dependent* relationships. Nor for arrogant, self-serving, *independent* relationships. Rather, He created us to enjoy well-rounded and wholesome *interdependent* relationships. Since He created us this way, we should settle for nothing less in our quest to solve the mystery of relationships.

CHAPTER 5

Relational Interdependence

Nor Dependence, Nor Independence, but Interdependence

One major clue in solving the mystery of relationships is our maturity level. Although you may have the urge to hurry life along, maturity takes time, growth, and proper progression. It comes through learning from life experiences and finding out who you are—spiritually, intellectually, emotionally, and physically. You may wonder, *Am I old enough to start dating?* or *Am I ready for a serious romantic relationship?* The answers to those questions lie in your ability to identify and interact within an *interdependent* relationship.

Interdependence means "depending on each other, unable to exist or survive without each other, and relying on mutual assistance, support, cooperation, or interaction."[26] In the context of personal relationships, consider these three levels of interaction:

- *Dependence:* wholly relying on someone else to meet basic needs
- *Independence:* solely relying on yourself to meet any needs
- *Interdependence:* mutual reliance and interaction in meeting shared needs and goals

Relational dependence works well in a parent-child relationship. The adult meets the needs of the child because the child is unable to meet those needs on her own. The adult has limited expectations for anything in return from the child. However, in a relationship between two adults, both of them lose in a dependent situation.

Immaturity in relationships shows up as being "too needy," emotionally insecure, or dependent on someone else for your self-image or self-worth. This level of interaction leaves the dependent person vulnerable to manipulation or coercion. It encourages the "If you love me, you will let me" pressure to physically compromise your moral standards to feel accepted, wanted, or loved. If you find yourself at this level, avoid getting involved in a relationship until you further develop yourself spiritually, intellectually, and emotionally.

Relational independence occurs when a person thinks he has no need of anything from anyone. An example would be a post-adolescent adult who is trying to break free from dependency on his parents. He considers himself to be self-reliant and believes he can get along just fine on his own with little or no help from anyone else. This independence may sound liberating, powerful, and fulfilling. However, finding fulfillment in isolation is not God's purpose for most people. Most of us have not been created for lonely independence. Nor is it what most people need or truly want.

This relational immaturity reveals itself in various forms. It may be a self-imposed protection against hurt from previous failed relationships. It may be a tough outer shell that covers your perceived inadequacies, low self-esteem, and poor self-image. It may show up as arrogance that hides your fear of trusting yourself to another person. Such independence leads to shallow, surface-level relationships. It encourages keeping people at a distance and restricts any potential core connection.

Relational interdependence involves two mature people welcoming each other into their lives to complete, fulfill, or complement what may be missing. In an interdependent relationship both people benefit because they find compatible fulfillment in each other. They recognize that each partner brings complementary value and strength to the relationship. They support and encourage each other. They grow together and promote ongoing personal development. They enjoy mutual trust, intimacy, affection, completion, fulfillment, and love.

> *Relational interdependence involves two mature people welcoming each other into their lives to complete, fulfill, or complement what may be missing.*

Picture a game of tennis between two equally gifted people, yet without the competition or the need for only one winner. Each person hits the ball to the other with the appropriate level of intensity to sustain the volley. If either person hits the ball harder or softer, or in a different direction, it lands in the net or out of bounds and the volley ends. Relational interdependence is the volley of life. The direction and intensity of each person's "hit" must be proportionately matched to sustain their life's "game."

In his book *The Seven Habits of Highly Effective People*, Stephen Covey describes the benefits of *interdependence*:

> *Life is, by nature, highly interdependent. To try to achieve maximum effectiveness through independence is like trying to play tennis with a golf club—the tool is not suited to the reality. Interdependence is a far more mature, more advanced concept. If I am physically interdependent, I am self-reliant and capable, but I also realize that you and I working together can accomplish far more than, even at my best, I could accomplish alone. If I am emotionally interdependent, I derive a great sense of worth within myself, but I also recognize the need for love, for giving,*

and for receiving love from others. If I am intellectually interdependent, I realize that I need the best thinking of other people to join with my own. As an interdependent person, I have the opportunity to share myself deeply, meaningfully, with others, and I have access to the vast resources and potential of other human beings.[27]

Is There One Special Person for Everyone?

Interdependence does not mean that you need someone to become the person God intends for you to be. God made you unique, with your own distinctive personality, needs, and life purpose. For this reason, it is important to develop and understand yourself *before* seriously pursuing or committing to a lifelong relationship. First develop the maturity to interact confidently at an interdependent level.

Life is like a huge puzzle. As you grow and develop, you are putting your life's puzzle together. Piece by piece you find out who you are. Your identity. Your moods. Your likes and dislikes. Emotional maturity. Food preferences and allergies. Morals and values. Taste in music. Personality traits. Hobbies. Fashion style. Career interests. Social circle and comfort level. As you put more of your puzzle together, you discover which pieces are missing and meant to be filled (or complemented) by someone else. Putting together as much of your puzzle as possible gives you the freedom to look for your "true fit" to complete the amazing picture of your life.

> When you "force fit" people into your life where they are not intended, you become distracted from your life's purpose.

When you "force fit" people into your life where they are not intended, you become distracted from your life's purpose. Filling a need in your life with an external "puzzle piece" instead of maturely developing that need on your own may cause you to miss your true fulfillment and completion. You may hold yourself back from achieving the ultimate design and unique purpose God has for you. For example, if you have a poor self-image, someone may make you feel wonderful with manipulative flattery or superficial compliments. But over time, as you grow and mature, you may find your "need" has been filled and your dependency on this person is no longer necessary. It is much better to develop yourself—in all four aspects—*prior to* becoming involved in a committed relationship.

God specializes in individual uniqueness. One example is the unique snowflakes He designs. They are insignificant and soon melt away, yet He makes each one with a specific pattern. Another example is each person's unmatched fingerprints. If God cares enough to deliberately create such uniqueness among the seemingly insignificant things, you can trust Him to help you find "the right one" to fit your relationship needs (Philippians 4:19). "Trust in the LORD and do good," ask Him for guidance, wait patiently for His timing, and He "will give you the desires of your heart" (Psalm 37:3-4, 7).

Solomon believed in relational uniqueness. He wrote, "Like an apple tree among the trees of the forest is my lover" (Song of Solomon 2:3), and, "My perfect one is unique" (Song of Solomon 6:9). One apple tree in the entire forest? That's quite unique! And "my perfect one"? Sounds like a special match to me.

Can I Live a Fulfilled Life and Remain Single?

Some people follow God's plan for their lives while staying single. Others may choose to stay single so they can follow their personal dreams and ambitions. The apostle Paul was unmarried. God's plan for him was to evangelize the world and devote his time and energy encouraging the many new Christian believers. In addition, he authored many of the books of the New Testament. It appears he did not have the time or interest for a romantic relationship. He recommended that people with similar calls of specific service for God should remain single as well. By not getting married, they can fully devote themselves to the will of God for their lives (I Corinthians 7:7-8).

If you sense God's call to perform a specific job or solo service that requires complete dedication, devote yourself fully to it. Finding your purpose in life brings personal contentment, a sense of accomplishment, and inner satisfaction. Before seriously looking for a potential spouse, prayerfully determine if you have a special calling. Until you figure this out, you do yourself a considerable disservice by getting romantically involved with anyone. You may be unable or unwilling to give the relationship and person the amount of affection, attention, and intensity they deserve. When this happens, you'll leave your partner unhappy, unfulfilled, unappreciated, and frustrated.

> Achieving and enjoying the completion, satisfaction, and fulfillment found in *interdependence* requires maturity.

By understanding the levels of relational maturity and interaction, we discover yet another clue in our quest to solve the mystery of relationships. Achieving and enjoying the completion, satisfaction, and fulfillment found in *interdependence* requires maturity—spiritually, intellectually, emotionally, and physically. We demonstrate this maturity by avoiding the pitfalls associated with *dependent* and *independent* relationships and by wisely pursuing an *interdependent* relationship.

CHAPTER 6

Made in God's Image

[handwritten annotation: The fact we are handmade in God's image gives us self esteem and enables us to have healthy interdependent relationships.]

Recognizing your tremendous value and developing a healthy sense of self-esteem will help you move beyond harmful *dependent* and detached *independent* relationships. Understanding who you are and respecting the astounding value God places upon you prepares you for a mature *interdependent* relationship.

You have been made in God's image. "God said, 'Let us make man in our image, after our likeness'" (Genesis 1:26 KJV). The pronouns *us* and *our* refer to God's plurality as the three distinct entities within the Holy Trinity. The Creation account confirms their presence and identifies their relational interaction. God the Father was present (John 1:1-2). The Holy Spirit moved upon the surface of the earth's waters (Genesis 1:2). Jesus (also called "the Word") created everything that was made (John 1:3). Although their specific assignments are not known, the phrase "let us make man" proves that all three worked on the project interdependently.

Before the first creative act began, the triune God held a cosmic meeting somewhere in the vast expanse of eternity past. During this meeting, the three of them discussed and coordinated their creative strategy. Matter was created from nothing. Expansive universes were crafted and hung in space. Miniscule atoms were designed. Unique DNA strands were built. Inviolable laws of gravity, physics, motion, aerodynamics, chemistry, and others were established. Planets were precisely located. Free will was granted—and sin was acknowledged.

> Talk about amazing love! Even before God created us, He saw our willful sinfulness and decided to continue with His creation plan anyway.

This divine meeting not only included every detail of creation. The plan of God's saving grace was also prepared at this time (II Timothy 1:9). God looked into eternity future, saw our sinful disobedience, and developed the plan of salvation. He did this to make it possible to restore our severed relationship with Him. Talk about amazing love! Even before God created us, He saw our willful sinfulness and decided to continue with His creation plan anyway.

Everything in creation was spoken into existence except man. It took a combined effort when God said, "Let us make man." Adam and Eve were *made*, not merely *spoken* into existence. This hands-on approach implies He was more intimately involved when He created us.

The awesome truth is that God personally handmade you. You are not the random product of some chance, evolutionary occurrence. According to Psalm 139:14, you have been "fearfully and wonderfully" made by God's own hand. Before pursuing a relationship with anyone, fully understand and accept your self-worth.

Genesis 1:26 says we are all created in God's *image* and *likeness*. Both words refer to similarity, resemblance, fashion, or manner. This does not mean we are similar to God in our characteristics or behaviors. The daily news reports that are filled with acts of selfishness, violence, deceit, and sin prove we are not similar to

God in behavior. Yes, there are occasional bright spots of human kindness and compassion, but they are far outnumbered by acts of human depravity. Since the initial fall of man (Genesis 3), sin has been passed along to every human being (Romans 5:12).

Humankind's inherent sinfulness is sufficient evidence that our "likeness" to God does not refer to His divine attributes. It simply means we are made in similar fashion, design, or components. One of the similarities to God's image is our relational design. We were made to enjoy healthy and fulfilling *interdependent* relationships. We should settle for nothing less.

CHAPTER 7

Incomplete Creation

Man is incomplete without a mate who he can be interdependent upon in the intellectual, emotional, and spiritual areas of life. The couple must understand what marriage is and prepare adequately for it.

God created each of us with the four aspects of life: spirit, mind, soul, and body. He formed Adam from the dust of the ground, providing him with a physical *body*. Then He breathed into him the breath of life (*spirit*). When this happened, man became a living—experiencing, sensing, feeling, emotional—being, or *soul* (Genesis 2:7). God also gave man a *mind* that provides the intellectual capacity for reasoning, decision making, and freewill choice.

As He did with all His previous phases of creation, God reviewed what He had done and saw that it was all good (Genesis 1:31). Everything was incredible!

With one small problem.

As God watched the first human being interact in His newly created, sinless, perfect environment, He knew Adam was missing something. Even with the four aspects of life given to him, Adam was incomplete. He was alone. God knew this and said, "It is not good that the man should be alone; I will make him an help-meet for him" (Genesis 2:18 KJV).

> God chose not to create man to exist alone or to be complete by himself. He made him in need of a "help meet."

In the midst of God's perfect earthly paradise, before the evil effects of sin, man was incomplete. *Did God make a mistake?* No. God chose not to create man to exist alone or to be complete by himself. He made him in need of a "help-meet."

Different Scripture versions define the term *help-meet* as a "suitable helper" (NIV), a "companion" (Msg), a "suitable partner" (CEV), and a "comparable helper" (NKJV). A combination of these terms gives us "compatible companion."

The obvious questions that arise are *A companion to do what? To help take care of God's new creation? To assist in caring for the animals, watering the plants, or feeding the fish? Just to be there? Merely as a partner for reproductive purposes?* These may all be components of God's overall relational plan. However, His intentions included something far greater and with a more intimate purpose.

God paraded all the animals in front of Adam and had him name each one, but none met his compelling need for companionship. Not one of them held the missing ingredient God knew was necessary for Adam's completion (Genesis 2:19-20). There was something so unique and complex about Adam that nothing in God's pristine and magnificent creation made him complete. He was still alone. Something inside him longed for more.

How could Adam be lonely in God's immediate presence? Because God created him as He created us—with the need for human interaction. We all require spiritual growth, intellectual engagement, emotional connection, and physical touch—relational interdependence. Adam did not have this since he was the lone human.

So God went back to His creative drawing board. The solution to Adam's need required a creature of complex components equal to his. Not exactly identical, yet not an exact opposite. Another "Adam" would be redundant and unnecessary, and would only multiply the missing component. An exact opposite may be attractive initially but would not have enough in common to sustain a long-term relationship.

God caused Adam to fall into a deep sleep. Then He performed the first donor surgery in the history of mankind. He took one of Adam's ribs (Genesis 2:21) and created a woman. Another human being created in God's image. She was equally granted the same four aspects of life as Adam: spirit, mind, soul, and body. Adam now had a comparable, suitable helper. His compatible companion.

God created Eve from Adam's side. Not from his head to dominate him. Not from his feet to serve him. Rather, from his side—near his heart. The organ from which life flows. The symbol from which love originates. Near to the core of human sentiment.

> God created Eve from Adam's side, near his heart, the core of human sentiment.

Upon their first meeting, Adam immediately acknowledged and accepted Eve as his "help-meet." The void he previously had was now satisfied (Genesis 2:23). It would not surprise us to hear Adam say something like *Way to go, God! Now, this is what I'm talkin' about!*

What made him react in this manner? Obviously, there were many interesting animals in God's creation from which to choose. Adam was familiar with them all as he'd just named them. Several were strong and could carry heavy burdens. Others were attractive, with varying colors and plumage. Many made cheerful and melodic sounds. Some were soft and cuddly, while others were humorous in their activities. Each one was splendid and instinctively gifted for God's creative purpose in its specific environment.

But none came close to filling Adam's inner void like Eve did.

When Eve walked up, his choice was clear. Something about her separated her from the rest of creation. In her presence, all else was secondary in importance and priority. His heart found its "home" with her.

There is no record in Scripture that either Adam or Eve needed any explanation, instruction, guidance, marriage counseling, couples retreat, or the latest book on relationships to respond and interact appropriately. Whatever commonalities and compatibility they found were given to them by God to achieve their mutual completion and fulfillment. They both had exactly what they needed to thrive together.

Only after their sinful disobedience did dysfunctional behavior enter the story. God's original design for their relationship didn't include that. He never intended for relationships to have incompatible or dysfunctional behavior. By His design, relational incompatibilities help us avoid relationships that will be harmful or unsatisfactory. God knew what He was doing with Adam and Eve, and He knows the unique requirements for successful relationships today.

There are some interesting points regarding this first human relationship that are important for us to recognize and accept if we are to solve the mystery of relationships.

Naked and Unashamed

Adam and Eve were both naked and unashamed (Genesis 2:25). Scripture does not say they shared spiritual insights, had a stimulating conversation, or were emotionally engaging. Instead, it emphasizes their physical appearance. One of the first recorded observations of male and female interaction was that both were naked, and they had no shame in being that way in each other's presence. They were completely vulnerable and exposed to each other and considered it perfectly normal.

This confirms God's initial intent that physical inhibitions have no part in a wholesome and inter-dependent marriage. When two people are married, it is perfectly natural for them to be naked

> Physical inhibitions have no part in a wholesome and interdependent marriage.

and unashamed with each other. It is absolutely appropriate and acceptable to be entirely exposed to each other and to express full enjoyment and satisfaction with each other that way.

Physical touch and sexual intimacy are critical elements to the human experience. A Mayo Clinic report confirms that physical intimacy affects feelings of wholeness and happiness.[28] There should be no inhibitions or shame in this level of interaction and interdependence.

Sure, you may say, *Adam and Eve had no inhibitions before their sinful fall. Now humanity is under the curse of sin and things are quite different.* But consider this. God cursed the ground and punished Adam and Eve for their disobedience; however, He did not curse their relationship. We should never use the excuse of sin's curse to tolerate dysfunctional, incompatible, or violent behavior in a relationship. Nor should we view it as an allowance for fear and inhibitions.

As you search for your compatible and lifelong partner, recognize that God fully intends for marriage to be based on compatibility, loving and respectful behavior, and interdependence in all four aspects of life. This leaves no place for anxiety or embarrassment.

Priority of the Relationship

Genesis 2:24 reveals the words typically recited in marriage ceremonies regarding a man leaving his father and mother and being joined to his wife. For whom was this initial message intended? Adam had no earthly parents to leave. God probably even had to explain the concept of parenthood to him. The best explanation for why this instruction is included at this precise moment may be to highlight the intimate involvement He intended for a man and woman to have in a vibrant and compatible marriage.

This instruction to place a high level of priority, significance, and commitment on the relationship is directed specifically toward Adam. But what about Eve? Are there similar instructions for her (and, by association, all women)?

Psalm 45 is a wedding song that illustrates the spiritual marriage of Christ and the church. However, it offers a parallel application for women. "Listen, O daughter, consider and give ear: forget your people and your father's house. The King is enthralled by your beauty; honor him" (verses 10-11). The same instruction to priority, significance, and commitment applies to both individuals in a relationship.

Does this mean newlyweds are to ignore or avoid all interaction with other relationships? Absolutely not. It simply confirms that a successful, interdependent relationship is to be sacred to the couple; other earthly relationships are to be secondary in importance. The significance and commitment of marriage must be clearly understood. A man may still be "mama's little boy" and a woman may still be "daddy's little girl." But upon getting married, the new couple should prioritize their relationship above all other human relationships.

No Ceremony Necessary

There is no record of an elaborate wedding ceremony that established Adam and Eve's union. No lengthy planning sessions. No arguments over the invitation list. No discussions about the size of the cake or the color coordination of the event. No bridesmaids or groomsmen. No bridal shower or bachelor party. No agonizingly long photo sessions. None of the traditional, formal events that create a traditional modern wedding ceremony (and that generate *huge* levels of stress for everyone involved). They did not need all that. They knew they were in a committed marriage for life.

This may challenge conventional thinking a bit, but it brings a few things into perspective. If the same amount of time, energy, effort, and planning given to the wedding *ceremony* were spent preparing for the *marriage,* there would be fewer divorces and unhappy marriages. A wedding ceremony is a beautiful occasion that marks the beginning of a couple's life together. It is a special time when family members and friends can celebrate the event with them. Stating vows before family, friends, and God gives formality to the couple's commitment. However, a marriage does not *need* a ceremony, because a wedding does not *make* a marriage. Only two things are essential to initiate a marriage: a man and a woman in full commitment and union (to meet God's requirements), and a properly completed and executed wedding license (to meet legal requirements).

Marriage is not merely a *tradition* in which a couple participates. It is not a romantic *ideal* that unites a couple. It is not an elaborate, rehearsed *event* that signifies their union. Marriage is personified by the people in it.

Long before the wedding ceremony, look closely at your prospective spouse—beyond the physical attraction. Take note of his morals, behaviors, habits, and lifestyles. View her through the lens of spending a lifetime together. Let the full realization sink in that together, *the two of you will be your marriage.*

From that perspective, marriages don't fail; people do. Marriages suffer when couples have a poor understanding of marriage or are not fully prepared for it. Marriages collapse when couples do not take enough time *before marriage* to discover whether incompatibilities exist. Many marriages fall apart because couples were not fully aware of or committed to everything marriage involves.

> Marriages don't fail; people do.

But marriages do not *have* to fall apart. Or even be strained. God never intended that when He created the concept of marriage.

He intended for each person to find and enjoy true compatibility spiritually, intellectually, emotionally, and physically.

To prepare for a satisfying, fulfilling, and lifelong marriage, patiently and fully develop yourself in all four aspects. You were created for human interaction and will feel the strong need to be accepted, to belong, and to be loved. But first, mature yourself to such a level so you fill your relational void in an interdependent way that honors God while also bringing true fulfillment to your life.

PREPARATION FOR DATING

You made my whole being;
you formed me in my mother's body.
I praise you because you made me in an
amazing and wonderful way.
What you have done is wonderful.
I know this very well.
You saw my bones being formed
as I took shape in my mother's body.
When I was put together there,
you saw my body as it was formed.
All the days planned for me
were written in your book
before I was one day old.
(Psalms 139:13–16, NCV)

CHAPTER 8

What's So Remarkable About the 4 Aspects?

All four aspects of life—spirit, mind, soul, and body—are God-given at the moment of conception. While you were still in your mother's womb (Psalm 139:13-16; Jeremiah 1:5; Job 31:15), they began shaping you in an amazingly complex manner. They form the distinctive person you become.

As you grow and mature, your spirit, mind, soul, and body are shaped and influenced by various internal and external factors. As a child, you developed through observing, experiencing, and learning. Development came at a graduated pace—first with parent(s) or primary caregivers, then with siblings or schoolmates, and ultimately with an expanded social network.

In his book *Cultures and Organizations: Software of the Mind*, Geert Hofstede confirms:

> *Values are mainly acquired during the first ten years of a child's life. They are absorbed by observation and imitation of adults and older children rather than by indoctrination. Every person carries within him or herself patterns of thinking, feeling, and potential acting which were learned throughout their lifetime. Much of it has*

been acquired in early childhood, because at that time a
person is most susceptible to learning and assimilating.[29]

Your individual rate and extent of development is influenced by numerous factors. Genes. Society. Culture. Personality traits and types. Standards of upbringing. Home environment. Observed parental behavior. Values. Beliefs. Life circumstances and personal choices. All these combined make you the unique individual you are.

Your developmental progress produces either a well-rounded, interdependent maturity in all four aspects or an immature imbalance where a deficiency in one or more aspects negatively affects your entire being. The complexity of all the influencing factors emphasizes the need to fully develop and balance all four aspects *before* you start looking for a compatible partner.

> An imbalance, overemphasis, or deficiency in any aspect creates a distortion in your life.

A successful and fulfilling relationship requires maturity, balance, and interdependence within all four aspects. An imbalance, overemphasis, or deficiency in any aspect creates a distortion in your life.

For example, if you place a fanatical focus on *spiritual* matters, you may become a stalwart person of faith, but you could rise so high into the "spiritual atmosphere" that you can't relate to other mere earthlings. If you spend the majority of your time on *intellectual* matters, you may become one of the smartest people in the world, but you could miss the incredible feelings and intimate connections in the world around you. A strict pursuit of *emotional* highs may be thrilling for a period of time, but it typically cycles to the dreaded emotional lows, which can result in mental depression and physical exhaustion. You may enjoy *physical* attractions and pleasures for the moment, but life is shallow when it is void of spiritual wisdom, intellectual discoveries, and emotional connections.

Sadly, many people do not seek balance in all four aspects of life. We normally choose to stay in our comfort zone of familiar behavior. Or we choose one aspect to the detriment of the others. For example, if a young woman focuses too intensely on her feelings and need for emotional connection, she may compromise her morals in the *physical* aspect. If she becomes emotionally attached to someone who is a negative influence in her life, she sets herself up to be manipulated and abused. If a young man chooses to engage in casual sex outside of marriage, he exposes himself to the potential negative consequences of unexpected pregnancy or sexual disease—along with the accompanying conflict within his spirit, mind, and soul.

Giving one aspect an improper emphasis generally leads to trouble. It can even result in a strained relationship. A sense of unfulfilled longing. A "settling" for lower expectations. Or the loss of the relationship altogether. For example, if two people are so overwhelmed by their physical attraction and emotional chemistry that they get married before truly getting to know each other, they may find themselves unfulfilled and incompatible in the other aspects. After prematurely fulfilling the *physical* aspect, they may regret having settled for the passion of the moment instead of wisely pursuing a wholesome relationship and fulfilling future.

Imagine two people who are drawn together by their spiritual strength and compatibility without identifying what they have in common in the other three aspects. If they get married, they may find their spiritual compatibility does not bring emotional or physical fulfillment. It was not intended to.

Each aspect is to be fully developed, equally applied, and abundantly enjoyed.

The bottom line is balance. Each aspect is to be fully developed, equally applied, and abundantly enjoyed.

It is easy to become "aspect imbalanced." Every day we are influenced by numerous sources that emphasize the individual importance of each aspect.

Churches, pastors, teachers, and counselors stress the importance of the *spiritual* aspect. Schools and other learning programs highlight the urgency of the *intellectual*. Personality tests and psychological assessments stress the importance of the *emotional*. Exercise programs, weight-loss advertisements, cosmetic firms, and plastic surgeons promote the appeal of the *physical*.

Developing each aspect of life is important. However, all four need to be fully matured and in harmony with each other. Recognizing their interdependence encourages maturity and balance in your life.

Each aspect has varying levels of depth or intensity. *Spiritual* levels may vary from that of a nonchalant seeker who dabbles in spiritual matters to that of a world-renowned evangelist who daily and fervently seeks God's throne of grace. *Intellectual* levels may vary from a relatively uneducated, simple person to a scholar devoted to ongoing academic achievements. *Emotional* levels may vary from a detached, unresponsive loner to an intimate, affectionate lover. *Physical* levels may vary from a realist who demonstrates little outward expression to a romantic whose mesmerizing kiss prolongs the passionate moment.

These varying levels are part of your individual uniqueness. They provide the opportunity for personal growth and the challenge of identifying your specific compatible mate. The goal is to find someone with a level and intensity in each aspect that is compatible with your own.

Even though everyone has all four aspects, some people do not fully *develop* each one. You may have natural tendencies to favor one aspect more than the others. You may have a deeper commitment to a particular aspect due to your career choice, personal preferences, or personality traits. But God gave you all four aspects to fully explore, experience, express, and enjoy. You need all four as you pursue the abundant life He intends for you to live (John 10:10 KJV).

Picture a juggler with four objects in the air. Each object must be given equal attention and concentration. This helps maintain the balance and rotation necessary to keep the act going. Any imbalance or distraction causes the objects to come crashing down and the act is over. Similarly, you must give each aspect your full and equal attention.

To measure the health of a potential relationship, answer these questions: "Will I be better off *spiritually* with this person in my life than I am without her? Will I be better off *intellectually*? What about *emotionally* and *physically*? If the person you are considering as a potential partner does not improve or complete you in all four aspects, she is probably not your compatible mate.

If you are in a relationship, ask yourself these questions: "Is the relationship one of mutual benefit, growth, completion, and fulfillment in all four aspects? Is it spiritually uplifting? Intellectually challenging? Emotionally fulfilling? Physically balanced?" If there is little or no mutual improvement or an inadequate balance in the four aspects for both partners, true compatibility may not exist.

However, if the answer to all these questions is a resounding "Yes!" for both partners, the relationship has true compatibility. Just as Adam became complete with Eve, two people in a well-matched relationship are better off together than when they were apart.

> Two people in a well-matched relationship are better off together than when they were apart.

Completing each other and meeting each other's needs must be mutual and reciprocal, leading to interdependency. Your partner may meet your needs; however, you have to meet your partner's needs as well. If not, this is a sign of aspect imbalance and incompatibility.

The four aspects of a relationship are like the four tires on a car. If one tire is out of balance or misaligned, you may arrive at your destination but the ride will not be smooth. Lack of proper attention and routine maintenance on any tire will lead to damage and you run the risk of a blowout. Now imagine the car with one tire missing. Even if the remaining three tires are well balanced, aligned properly, and contain the proper air pressure, you are still headed for a wreck.

> Both people in a relationship should each have their four aspects fully developed and then mutually shared at compatible levels and intensity.

Likewise, in a romantic relationship the *presence* and compatible *balance* of all four aspects are required. To achieve true fulfillment in an interdependent relationship, both people should each have their four aspects fully developed and then mutually shared at compatible levels and intensity.

Consider each aspect separately. When you fully understand each one, then pursue full maturity and development in all four. After that, learn to accurately evaluate the aspects in other people. This will help you identify your potential for compatibility with a prospective mate.

CHAPTER 9

Excuse Me, But Your Spirit Is Showing

When the word "spiritual" is mentioned, what comes to your mind? Religion and "holier than thou" hypocrites? Movies about angels, demons, ghosts, or other unexplained paranormal events? For our consideration, the spiritual aspect of life includes moral standards, ethics, and religious beliefs.

The Significance of Your Spirit

God is "the God of the spirits of all mankind" (Numbers 27:16). Our spirits came from Him. This component was "breathed into" all of us when God created Adam (Genesis 2:7). He set humans apart from the rest of His creation by giving us this immortal element.

The spirit is your vertical window that enables your awareness of God and who He is.[30] It is that part of you that makes you cry out to

> The spirit is your vertical window that enables your awareness of God and allows you to establish an intimate relationship with Him.

God for help when you are in trouble or danger. By your spirit you can establish an intimate relationship with Him, communicate with Him, and worship Him.

Of all the aspects, the *spiritual* aspect has the longest-lasting impact. God is a Spirit (John 4:24) and He is eternal (Revelation 1:8). Because of this life-giving element that He gave you, your spirit is also eternal. This means you will live forever. Where? Only two eternal destinations are identified in the Bible: heaven and hell. God leaves the final choice to you.

You may either accept or reject God's Son, Jesus Christ, as your personal Lord and Savior. This is how you enter into a personal relationship with Him. If you accept Him, your spirit is reborn. Jesus described this spiritual rebirth as being born again (John 3:3, 7). This rebirth offsets the spiritual death that has been passed along to all humanity by Adam's sinful disobedience (Romans 5:12). Those who accept Christ will spend eternity in heaven with God. Those who don't, have only one other eternal destination.

Some people doubt the existence of the *spiritual* aspect. Their thought is, *If it cannot be seen, it must not exist.* However, just because we can't see or choose not to believe in something doesn't change its reality. Not many people have seen a million dollars, but we don't deny such a thing exists. We may not be able to see oxygen, but that doesn't mean it is not in the air all around us. Nor does it change our reliance on it for ongoing life. We can't see the wind, but we hear the sound it makes. We see its effect on the trees, clouds, and other objects (John 3:8). Sometimes, in order to see something not readily visible to our eyes, we have to look at its effect, impact, or influence.

Anyone who attends a funeral, or has seen a dead body, will notice that something is dramatically different about the deceased. Something is missing. The physical shell no longer looks the same. That missing "something" is the spirit of life. It is by and with the breath of God (the spirit) that we have life (Job 27:3).

When "the spirit returns to God who gave it" (Ecclesiastes 12:7), the physical body dies (James 2:26).

Upon His death on the cross, Jesus surrendered His spirit back to God the Father. With His last breath He said, "Father, into your hands I commit my spirit" (Luke 23:46). For those who have placed their trust in Christ, the natural separation of body and spirit at death results in being "absent from the body" and immediately and forever in God's presence (II Corinthians 5:6-8 KJV).

Without a sound spiritual foundation, you will have deficiencies and imbalances in your mind, soul, and body. Think of it this way. No matter what sport you play, there are rules and boundary lines. The better you know the rules, the more prepared you are to play the game. When you understand the purpose of the boundary lines, the game makes more sense. The moral standards, ethics, and religious beliefs included in the *spiritual* aspect establish the guidelines for a wholesome and interdependent life.

> Without a sound spiritual foundation, you will have deficiencies and imbalances in your mind, soul, and body.

Spiritual Interaction with the Other Three Aspects

You may be thinking, *How does learning about the spiritual aspect help me with my personal relationships? How will it help me get a date and find my compatible mate?*

Society has done a tremendous job of downplaying or disregarding the *spiritual* aspect of life. Religion and personal beliefs are among the taboo topics that also include politics and personal income. However, we can link most negative relationship statistics to a spiritual imbalance or immaturity. Sexual experimentation, exploitation and abuse, teenage pregnancy, abortion, divorce— most are directly tied to a spiritual deficiency or imbalance.

The fulfilling life you desire, including finding that special some-

> The *spiritual* aspect provides the *moral framework* for the other three aspects.

one, requires that you fully develop and balance all four aspects. You can't ignore one and think it won't negatively affect your life. As you develop maturity and balance in all four, you will find that the *spiritual* aspect plays a large role in your relational interaction. It provides the *moral framework* for the other aspects.

Intellectually

Scripture instructs us to put on the mind of Jesus Christ (Philippians 2:5) and to be transformed by the renewing (refreshing or repairing) of our minds (Romans 12:2). It also says God's Holy Spirit will lead us into all truth (John 16:13).

[handwritten margin note: The Spirit indwelling our minds]

A mature and balanced *spiritual* aspect gives you the moral basis for the decisions you make in life. By "putting on" the mind of Jesus, you approach your life's choices from His perspective. You align your relationship standards according to the morality outlined in God's Word. This includes where to go on a date, what to do on a date, and what type of physical involvement is acceptable before marriage.

The truth of God's Word never changes (Psalm 119:89; Matthew 24:35). Therefore, you can trust what it says and not try to manipulate it to your own preferences and desires, or the latest cultural fads. The only accurate mindset is the one that aligns with God's Word.

Emotionally

Uncontrolled emotions may cause you to think and do things contrary to what God intends. For example, imagine you are extremely attracted to someone who is not your spouse. You experience such overwhelming feelings that you want to run into that person's arms and let romantic passion consume you both.

If (prior to marriage) you do not control these feelings with your *spiritual* aspect, you may forget all about your morals and behavioral standards.

A mature and balanced *spiritual* aspect helps you govern your emotions to allow only what is appropriate for the specific relational stage of your life. When someone breaks your heart, you can take comfort in knowing God still loves you and wants the best for you (Jeremiah 29:11). When you are lonely and feeling desperate, you can find solace in knowing He will never leave you or abandon you (Hebrews 13:5). When you are overwhelmed with guilt for something you have done wrong, you can claim His forgiveness and cleansing (I John 1:9). When you experience the happiness and satisfaction of a fulfilling relationship, you can express your gratitude to God for blessing you with such a wonderful gift (James 1:17). Using God's Word as your spiritual guide helps you avoid unnecessary emotional distress and imbalance.

Physically

A mature and balanced *spiritual* aspect helps you understand why sexual involvement is reserved for marriage. It also allows the freedom of full physical expression after marriage. Having a biblically based spiritual framework brings safety and security to the *physical* aspect.

God's Word confirms that all sexual involvement must wait for marriage (Hebrews 13:4; I Corinthians 7:9). It also assures us that there is no need to be embarrassed, timid, or fearful of sexual interaction within marriage. "Perfect [complete] love drives out fear" (I John 4:18, brackets added). Scripture also encourages us to be bold (Joshua 1:9), and to not have a fearful spirit (II Timothy 1:7). This courage and confidence applies not only to the *spiritual* aspect, but to the others as well—including the *physical.*

As you apply God's Word to your life, the *spiritual* aspect affects the other three. Intellectually, your thoughts and decisions change. Emotionally, you sense and feel things differently. Physically, your

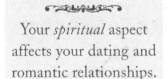

Your *spiritual* aspect affects your dating and romantic relationships.

habits and lifestyle align with your moral standards. You go places, do things, and say things that are different from those who are at a lower level of spiritual development. Because of this, your *spiritual* aspect affects your dating and romantic relationships.

How the *Spiritual* Aspect Affects Relationships

This aspect should be one of the first topics of any dating discussion. If the other person is not a Christian, it should be the first sign that she is not compatible with you. Continued discussion or future dating activities should be discouraged.

If a potential mate claims to be a Christian, observe his behaviors. Ask about her moral standards. Ask how he became a Christian. If her lifestyle or answers do not align with scriptural morality, do not pursue a relationship level beyond casual friendship.

The difference between believers and unbelievers should be as noticeable as between night and day. There is no compatibility between light and darkness (I John 1:5-7). When you turn off a room's light after nightfall, the room is immediately plunged into darkness. No section of the room is half light and half dark. There is no happy compromise between the two. Such is the spiritual difference between a believer and an unbeliever. They have different priorities, beliefs, values, and convictions. And opposite eternal destinations.

Paul warns Christians not to be "unequally yoked [paired] together with unbelievers" (II Corinthians 6:14 NKJV, brackets added). He illustrates this relational imbalance using two different kinds of animals yoked together in the same harness. Imagine a kangaroo and a lion attached to the same harness. Though joined together, they will have very different agendas. They will not head in the same direction. They will not pull the same weight. The strain on each animal will be noticeable.

The same holds true for two spiritually incompatible people. If one person is a dedicated Christian with a "hunger and thirst for righteousness" (Matthew 5:6) while the other person, though claiming to be a Christian, routinely engages in bad habits or sinful behavior, their relational strain will be quite obvious.

An "unequally yoked" or incompatible relationship will not provide the satisfaction, fulfillment, and interdependence most people long for and that God intends. No matter the physical attraction, intellectual inspiration, and emotional chemistry, if the *spiritual* aspect is not compatible, any effort to build true and lasting relational harmony will be ultimately ineffective (Psalm 127:1).

A morally strong *spiritual* aspect governs relational behavior. It affects the *mind* by controlling thoughts, fantasies, and lustful ideas. It affects the *soul* by controlling intense passions, the strong desire for connection, and powerful feelings. It affects the *body* by controlling the relational behavior while dating, the physical affection level, and what is allowed to be said and done. After marriage, the *spiritual* aspect lifts these controls and allows the freedom of full expression in all four aspects.

> A morally strong *spiritual* aspect governs relational behavior.

Spiritual Development and Maturity

God's Word does more than help you choose your eternal destination. It also guides you while living here on earth. God intended it to be a resource for your spiritual development. The Bible has the power to penetrate your thoughts and the attitudes of your heart (Hebrews 4:12). It is the only book that is alive! According to Paul, it was "divinely breathed" by God (II Timothy 3:16).

After your spirit is "born again," it must be fed and strengthened to maturity. Ongoing spiritual nourishment is required to strengthen your spirit just as food and exercise strengthen your body, as maturity and experience strengthen your emotions, and as continual learning strengthens your mind.

To develop and mature spiritually, read God's Word daily and apply it to your everyday life. Living according to God's Word helps us stay morally pure (Psalm 119:9). The Bible is a lamp for our feet and a light for our path (Psalm 119:105). It provides us with:

- Instant illumination (for each step of life's pathway)
- Ongoing illumination (for all of life's journey)

As you read God's Word, you receive what you need today. Tomorrow's light will build on today's. This is the way you receive ongoing enlightenment and direction.

In addition to reading God's Word, applying it to your life, and having regularly scheduled quiet times of prayer with God, you strengthen your *spiritual* aspect by worshiping God and having fellowship with other Christians.

Although worship and fellowship can take place anywhere, most often it occurs at church. Regular church attendance demonstrates your faithfulness and reveals on whose team you belong. If you were on a professional sports team, you would be expected to attend the meetings, practice sessions, and games. Imagine how foolish you would look if you said you were on the team and expected to be paid, but never showed up for any team activities (if you had the ability to do so). It's equally foolish to claim to be a Christian and expect God's blessings, but never show up at church or participate in any of the activities and events.

You worship God by praising Him through music, personal testimony of thanksgiving for His many blessings, and showing reverence when you come into His presence. Worship is a means of connecting with God in the spiritual realm.

When you fellowship (interact) with other Christians, you are sharing a sense of community. When you gather with other believers to share, support, and encourage each other, you connect with God's people spiritually, intellectually, emotionally, and physically.

When you are dating, make sure you include prayer and Bible reading in your activities. This may not happen on a first date. But as the relationship grows, this should be an included activity. Doing this helps keep the dating behavior honorable. It reminds you that God is watching. It helps you acknowledge that God should be involved in your relationship. And it prepares you for future family devotional time.

Signs of Spiritual Maturity

Here are some ways of demonstrating growth and personal maturity in the *spiritual* aspect:

- *Establish a personal relationship with God.* This involves being spiritually "reborn" by placing your faith in Jesus Christ as your Lord and Savior. This decision is far more important than when or how or who to start dating. Eternity awaits your decision—and all of heaven will rejoice when you are spiritually reborn (Luke 15:7).
- *Know what you believe and why you believe it.* Spiritual maturity is not simply mimicking what your parents, grandparents, or others believe. It is fully understanding your religious beliefs and why you believe them. Having this solid understanding helps to answer any questions, doubts, or temptations you may encounter. As Christians, we are to "always be prepared to give an answer to everyone who asks you to give the reason for the hope that you have" (I Peter 3:15).
- *Have a well-defined set of dating standards that align with God's Word.* This includes your predetermination not to date an unbeliever. It also includes your commitment to not perform or allow any sexual actions prior to marriage. The counsel

Peter gives is to "be holy in all your conduct" (I Peter 1:15, ESV). Establish your moral boundaries before you start dating. Create a list of morally acceptable behaviors—then stick to it. In the "heat of the moment" is not the time to figure out what is morally acceptable and how you should behave.

- *Courageously stand for your convictions—even if you must stand alone.* Develop the ability to withstand negative peer pressure. Even if everyone around you is engaging in immoral behavior, hold firmly to your convictions. Solomon's counsel is "If sinners entice you [tempt; charm; pressure], do not give in to them" (Proverbs 1:10, brackets added). Stand firm even if your friends ridicule you or try to influence you. Even if doing so costs you a relationship with the "hottest" person in your world.

- *Maintain a positive self-image and acceptance as one of God's valuable, handmade creations.* This will help you avoid the "smooth talkers" who prey on the vulnerabilities and insecurities of others (Proverbs 7:21). They use flattery to make you feel better about yourself. They say "all the right things" that make you feel loved and accepted. But their intentions are to take advantage of you. Protect yourself against their subtle attack by basing your self-worth on what God says about you. You are His wonderful creation (Psalm 139:14). You are incredibly loved as one of His children (I John 3:1). You are an heir to His coming kingdom (Romans 8:17). You are a child of the King of Kings! (Rev 17:14).

Spiritual Compatibility Questionnaire

Here are some questions to consider when determining the spiritual expectations you have for a potential spouse. Be mindful of these questions (and others you may add to the list) during the initial discovery with your dating partner. Allow them to help you determine his or her spiritual level. Use them to help identify *spiritual* common ground as well as differences. Let them serve as the moral framework for your dating activities. Apply them to your relational pursuit in a way that honors God and is personally rewarding.

1. Is your relationship spiritually compatible? Or are you "unequally yoked"? What evidence has your dating partner given that confirms she is a Christian? How comparable are your views on spiritual development (Bible reading and studying, dedicated prayer time, applying what you learn to your life, etc.)?

2. What moral standards have you set for dating? How do your moral standards compare to those of your dating partner? In what ways do you encourage each other's spiritual development and growth?

3. Do each of you hold your moral standards, beliefs, and values as true convictions or mere preferences depending on the situation or circumstances? Do you hold firm to your convictions or do you retreat when faced with pressure or challenges? Think of a time when you observed your dating partner handle a tough situation by staying true to his convictions.

4. Do you each know *what* you believe and *why* you believe it? How do your views compare on doctrinal issues? How do your views compare regarding regular church attendance? How similar is your commitment to being involved in church ministry? Do both of you model compatible values, morals, behaviors, attitudes, and habits that you want to display to your future children?

5. When life's challenges, difficulties, and setbacks come, how do your reactions compare? Do you each draw on your spiritual strength in handling conflict, pressure, resistance, or uncertainty?

CHAPTER 10

Keep Your Mind in Mind

Have you ever thought, *I don't know why I need to learn algebra—I'll never use it in life?* Well, it may surprise you to know that even algebra relates to personal relationships. The underlying concept of algebra trains your mind to perform deductive reasoning on a set of unknown variables to solve an equation. This same process applies to life.

Through deductive reasoning, your mind processes various scenarios to arrive at a logical conclusion. It teaches you the law of *if* and *then*. *If* you touch a hot stove, *then* you will be burned. *If* you study your homework, *then* you will be prepared for the test. Your choices and decisions have rewards and consequences.

> Your choices
> and decisions
> have rewards and
> consequences.

The same deductive reasoning applies to dating and your search for a compatible spouse. *If* you allow hormones, attraction, and chemistry to control your dating behavior, *then* you run the risk of getting pregnant, catching a sexually transmitted disease, and/ or having emotional issues. However, *if* you align your physical attraction and emotional chemistry with your spiritual morality and intellectual reason, *then* you are living a mature and balanced life that God can bless.

The Significance of Your Mind

God created you with intellectual capacity so you can learn *about* Him and *from* Him. You gain understanding and wisdom as you interact with Him and within His creation. Your mind gives you the ability to think, reason, evaluate, and understand. You use your mind to make choices based on a set of criteria. You can also determine the probable outcomes of your decisions. Your mind is where you determine how to exercise your free will.

Until you mature intellectually, you will make irrational, risky, and sometimes foolish decisions. These poor decisions lead you to make harmful and regrettable choices. For example, as a young child you may have wanted to stick a key into an electrical outlet. This harmful decision makes no sense to an intellectually mature adult who knows the danger and regret associated with your choice. Your parents' knowledge and experience with electricity protected you—even though you threw a temper tantrum for not getting your way.

> Without a sound intellectual foundation or rational decision-making ability, well-informed and wise choices are generally not made.

Without a sound intellectual foundation or rational decision-making ability, well-informed and wise choices are generally not made. For this reason, we should constantly pray along with King David, "May the words of my mouth and the meditation of my heart be pleasing in your sight, O Lord" (Psalm 19:14). The word *heart* in this verse refers to a person's feelings, will, and intellect.[31] You should so guard your *intellectual* aspect that your thoughts and decisions (including those about your dating or romantic relationships) are acceptable from God's viewpoint.

The New Testament writer James gives the warning that "a double *minded* man is unstable in *all* his ways" (James 1:8 KJV, italics added). Developing your mind gives you the ability to make wise decisions and stick to them. People who are constantly changing their minds are hesitant and indecisive in their mental thought processes. This instability carries over into relationships. One day they like a person, the next day they don't. Today they think someone is "hot;" tomorrow, not so much. Until you develop a mature *intellectual* aspect, your "likes" and "loves" will change daily.

Paul encourages us to "take captive every *thought* to make it obedient to Christ" (II Corinthians 10:5, italics added). We are to deliberately control our thoughts. When you start fantasizing immorally about someone, control those thoughts with the *spiritual* aspect. Ask yourself what Christ would think about your fantasies. Ask for His forgiveness for such thoughts and do not dwell on them. The longer you contemplate impure thoughts and mental images, the greater the risk that you will act on them.

Your mind stores your memories not just for your lifetime, but also into eternity. Luke 16:19-31 relates a story Jesus told of a rich man and a beggar named Lazarus. Both men died. Lazarus went to heaven. The rich man was tormented in hellish flames. Even after his physical death, the rich man's mind was still working. He recognized Abraham. He remembered Lazarus. He knew and felt pain. He remembered his brothers who were still alive on earth and their sinful lifestyles. When he asked Abraham for mercy from his torment, Abraham told him to "remember" (Luke 16:25). His mind was drawn back to his earthly life and the choices he made.

Pretend for a moment that you could download all your memories into a computer. As you review each memory, are there any you want to delete? How many poor choices do you wish you could

> The choices you make and the memories you create remain stored in your mind for eternity.

send to the recycle bin? Admittedly, doing so would be a welcome relief. However, that is not the reality of life. The choices you make and the memories you create remain stored in your mind for eternity. Your goal should be to control your thoughts and behaviors in such a way that you create pleasant memories. Memories you can share with anyone. Memories you cherish forever, not ones you will always regret.

Making daily decisions with eternity in mind will have a significant effect on your relational pursuit. Asking, *How will this decision look when I stand before God?* should help you make less impulsive choices. When faced with the temptation to compromise your moral standards, think it through to the end result. Casual flirting can lead to hugging, hugging may lead to fondling, fondling may then lead to sexual caressing, which leads to premarital sex, which eventually leads to negative consequences. Ask yourself, *How will my actions look to my friends and family?* Filter your thoughts and actions through the moral framework of your *spiritual* aspect.

Intellectual Interaction with the Other Three Aspects

> Physical attraction and emotional chemistry must be balanced and aligned with spiritual morality and intellectual wisdom.

Strengthening your mind is an act of self-protection against impulsive urges, temptations, and vulnerabilities you experience in the other three aspects of life. Physical attraction and emotional chemistry are wonderful elements of a relationship. But they must be balanced and aligned with spiritual morality and intellectual wisdom.

The *intellectual* aspect is interdependent with the other three. When you are deficient in one or overemphasizing another, your reasoning capacity is impaired. Allowing one aspect (for instance, the *physical*) to dominate your thoughts can destroy your life. Samson is an example of this (Judges 14).

From his birth, Samson was chosen by God to deliver the Israelites from their oppressive enemy, the Philistines. God gave specific instructions to Samson's parents regarding how they should raise him and what he could and could not do. Based on what happened in his life, he didn't listen very well to God's instructions or to his parents' experienced and loving counsel.

On one of his visits to an enemy city, Samson saw a young Philistine woman. She appealed to his overemphasized and uncontrolled physical desires. Without even speaking with her, he returned home and urged his parents to "get her for me as my wife" (Judges 14:2). His parents tried to change his mind. After all, she was the enemy! *Samson, what are you thinking?* Who in their right mind wants to date—much less marry—one of his enemies? His parents tried to reason with him by encouraging him to find a more suitable wife among his own people. But he showed his stubbornness (and his intellectual immaturity) by defiantly saying, "She's the right one for me" (Judges 14:3).

A few verses later, he actually talks with her. And likes her! In a very short time, he marries her. Nevertheless, his lack of wisdom and his rebellion against logical advice leads to a disastrous ending. He loses her as his wife. She ends up losing her life. Samson's intellectual deficiency ultimately cost him his life too. All because he allowed a physical imbalance to overrule his spiritual morality and his intellectual wisdom.

The *intellectual* aspect provides the *reasoning capacity* for the other three aspects.

The *intellectual* aspect provides the *reasoning capacity* for the other three aspects.

Spiritually

A sound mind gives rational and unbiased insight into a person's character, morals, motives, convictions, beliefs, intentions, and moral boundaries. The prophet Jeremiah poses this rhetorical question: "Can leopards change their spots?" (Jeremiah 13:23, NIRV). Anyone can improve his behavior for a short time, especially while dating. It takes time and a variety of situations to reveal a person's true character and motives. Use your mind to objectively observe your dating partner's behaviors and lifestyle.

One great use of your mind is to help determine your life's purpose. If God has called you to be a missionary to a foreign land, it's not smart to be in a relationship with someone who doesn't have that same calling. If your dream job is in Dallas, Texas, it makes no sense to become involved with someone who lives in New York City. You may be mutually attracted and emotionally connected; however, if you decide to marry a person with a different life purpose, you will live with a perpetual dilemma. Should you follow your calling and pull the other person along where she hasn't been called? Or should you turn your back on God's purpose for your life (or even your personal ambitions) so you can be more attentive to your spouse's needs and desires?

> A wise strategy is to identify your life's purpose *before* getting involved in a relationship.

A wise strategy is to identify your life's purpose *before* getting involved in a relationship. It helps you stay true to yourself while looking for someone who matches your life's purpose and goals.

Emotionally

Intellectual reason should objectively balance out emotional passion. Use your mind to analyze your feelings and their source. Instead of just enjoying intense feelings about someone, ask yourself, *Why do I feel the way I do? What attracts me to this person? Does this relationship make sense?* Look beyond what your heart wants to see and hear—use your mind. Objectively assess the depth and potential of the relationship. Confirm that the relationship is balanced in all four aspects and is not simply physical in nature. Instead of getting caught up in the whirlwind of your emotions, assess the other person's capacity for emotional connection. Determine if your dating partner is emotionally "available" and willing to positively express healthy emotions.

Physically

Your mind evaluates physical attraction. It identifies and interprets various methods of communication, including verbal words and nonverbal body language. It observes clues regarding facial expressions and visible behavioral traits. Your mind helps you decide which actions your body will carry out. For this reason, your *spiritual* aspect must govern your mind.

Paul instructs us to *think* about things that are true, honest, just, pure, lovely, of good report, virtuous, and praiseworthy (Philippians 4:8). To have a deep level of connection and compatibility in your relationship, find a person who is "like-minded"—someone who also has the mind of Christ and who allows the *spiritual* aspect to control her actions. Someone who is *true* to his word. *Honest* in feelings and intentions. *Pure* in thoughts and actions. As *lovely* on the inside as she is outwardly. Someone with an honorable reputation. Keep these thoughts in mind as you look for your potential spouse. And remember, he or she should be looking for the same in you.

How the *Intellectual* Aspect Affects Relationships

Intellectual compatibility is often the first step in developing a relationship. When you meet someone, you both try to find things you have in common. You also identify differences. What you talk about depends on the level of intellectual similarities and interest. If enough mutual interest exists, and as the comfort level grows, you each share information that is closer to your vulnerable core.

Generally, a more developed mind makes it easier to talk and express thoughts and feelings clearly. This does not mean both people have to be geniuses to have a successful relationship. Nor does it mean that people at different intellectual levels cannot be compatible. Varying intellectual levels provide the opportunity for learning and growth. However, a significant intellectual gap may limit the things you have in common. More misunderstandings may occur and the potential for embarrassing or confrontational situations may increase.

For example, imagine two people in a relationship who have different thoughts regarding money management. If one person has an impulsive "spend it if you got it" mindset while the other has a frugal "save it for later" outlook, they will probably experience ongoing struggles.

Another example would be if two people wrote each other love letters. One is well thought out, deeply expressive from the heart, and uses generally accepted grammar and punctuation. The other is written in multi-colored crayons and contains surface-level thoughts, run-on sentences, and spelling errors. The intended messages of both letters are lost due to their intellectual difference.

Differences in the *intellectual* aspect restrict the ability to hold meaningful conversations and share similar life stories. What if a highly educated, well-traveled woman saw a beautiful painting in an art museum in Europe and tried to describe it to someone who had never left his small hometown, not received an advanced education, and found artistic beauty in the soda-can sculpture he created? When she tells him the painting is invaluable, he may think that means it has no value at all.

> For relational compatibility, find someone at generally the same intellectual level as your own.

If you are looking for relational compatibility, find someone at generally the same intellectual level as your own. This will provide common ground from which you can grow together.

Intellectual Development and Maturity

Intellectual development and maturity occur gradually as you grow older and gain more knowledge, wisdom, and exposure to life's experiences. This gradual progression is necessary. A child's mind is not ready to understand complex concepts. Everyone needs time to gradually develop the ability to understand deeper thoughts and situations.

Until your mind is mature and capable of sound reasoning, rely on the advice and counsel of trusted sources such as adult family members, guidance counselors, psychologists, or pastors. Minds that are still "under construction" can find great benefit from other people's knowledge, wisdom, and experience. Their seasoned point of view can protect you as your mind matures. Their reasoning can rescue you when your mind is blinded by subjective imbalances or deficiencies in the other aspects.

Imagine an inexperienced group of hikers who want to go for a long hike in the mountains. If they're smart, they will take along an accurate map, hire an experienced guide, or get specific instructions from people who are familiar with the chosen trail. Choosing not to do this increases their risk of getting lost or encountering danger along the trail.

The good news is, you have all the resources you need for your hike through the mountains of life. The Bible is your map, Jesus is your guide, and there are experienced adults around you who have already traveled the early trail of life. Their journey may have included getting lost a time or two, and they may have the scars from falling over a few cliffs, but you can learn from their experience and avoid the mistakes they've made.

Knowledge, wisdom, and experience are all elements of the *intellectual* aspect. They work together to support the reasoning capacity

Knowledge, wisdom, and experience are all elements of the *intellectual* aspect.

of the mind. Solomon says, "The LORD gives wisdom, and from his mouth come knowledge and understanding" (Proverbs 2:6). Solomon also explains some of the benefits of having wisdom:

> *Wisdom will control your mind, and you will be pleased with knowledge. Sound judgment and good sense will watch over you. Wisdom will protect you from evil schemes and from those liars who turned from doing good to live in the darkness. (Proverbs 2:10-13,* CEV*)*

Knowledge is your lifelong accumulated learning—what you know. *Wisdom* is "judging rightly and following the soundest course of action, based on knowledge, experience, and understanding."[32] You show your wisdom by appropriately applying what you know to your life. *Experience* is "the act of living through an event or events; the effect on a person of anything or everything that has happened to that person."[33] It involves actually living through any successes and failures. *Maturity* is learning from life experiences (your own as well as other people's) and choosing not to repeat the same mistakes.

Consider the following scenarios as we apply these four intellectual tools:

- *Knowledge* tells you dating is fun, sex is pleasurable, and there are many attractive people in the available "dating pool."
- *Wisdom* tells you dating is a way to get to know people and learn how to interact with them, premarital sex is immoral, and physical beauty may only be skin deep.
- *Experience* tells you dating is a time to discover commonalities and differences, premarital and casual sex are not only immoral but also shallow and risky and come with a high price, and a person's inner beauty may be more important than being good looking.
- *Maturity* tells you dating should involve discovering compatible levels in all four aspects of life, sex is intended for the sanctity and safety of marriage, and beauty is the shared and

wholesome attraction of two people who cultivate a perpetually romantic lifetime together.

Signs of Intellectual Maturity

Here are some ways of demonstrating growth and maturity in the *intellectual* aspect:

- *Allow the truth from God's Word to affect your decisions.* God gave you a mind and He expects you to develop it and use it to make good decisions and choices. Apply the wisdom from God's Word to your reasoning process. Learn all you can. Jesus said, "Diligently study the Scriptures" (John 5:39). Find additional truth and wisdom about relationships. Since your "steps" are directed by the Lord (Proverbs 20:24), use God's Word to identify the life purpose He has for you.
- *Develop the reasoning skills to make sound decisions based on reliable sources.* Avoid making decisions based on what everyone else is doing or on surveys found in popular worldly magazines. Peer groups may not be the best source of reliable advice—after all, their life experiences are not much different from your own.
- *Ask questions and keep an open mind to feedback from trusted mentors and family members.* Never be embarrassed or afraid to ask the relationship questions you have. There are experienced adults all around you who are willing to answer. Seeking advice from wise sources keeps you safe (Proverbs 11:14). A good process for finding the best guidance is from the Bible first, reliable adults second, deductive reasoning third, and then your personal preference.
- *Take full responsibility for your decisions and actions—for both the rewards and the consequences.* When you make decisions, you can normally choose the rewards, but not the consequences. If you make a bad decision, do not shift the blame to others or look for the easy way out. Always keep in mind that "each of us will give an account of himself to God" (Romans 14:12). God sees everything you do and there is no shifting of blame

with Him. The key is to make a wise decision from the start. When young Daniel was taken prisoner to Babylon, from the moment he arrived, he "purposed in his heart" to stay true to his religious faith (Daniel 1:8, KJV). He was in a foreign land far from home—who would blame him for trying to "fit in"? But he made the right decision, stood by it, and God blessed him.

- *Learn continuously.* Make a habit of continually developing your mind. Read books about your favorite hobbies, read the Bible, read Christian books (fiction and nonfiction). If you are not fond of reading, listen to audio books. Participate in diverse blogs to respectfully defend or enhance your point of view. Study topics beyond those related to your career. Keep yourself informed of current world events. These activities will increase your *intellectual* aspect and provide you with more things to talk about with a dating partner.

- *See the world.* Broaden your intellectual horizons by traveling outside the area around your home. There is comfort in staying in your hometown; however, there are also limitations. Part of your development should include observing different personalities in different settings. Travel throughout your state, then take a trip across the country. If possible, journey to another country. Learn different cultures. Meet different people. Expand your perspective on the world.

Intellectual Compatibility Questionnaire

Here are some questions to consider when discovering the intellectual expectations you have for a dating partner. Honest answers to these questions, as well as those you add to the list, should be part of the intellectual discovery of your dating process. They should help identify the *intellectual* level of your partner as well as your commonalities and differences. Questions like these enhance your reasoning ability for your dating activities. Remember to filter the answers through the moral framework of your *spiritual* aspect.

1. Do you share the same interests as your dating partner, or are you constantly trying to *like* what the other person deeply enjoys? Do you participate in these activities only to make a good impression? Are they things you would consider doing for life?

2. Do both of you know God's purpose for your lives? Is God's plan for your life compatible with His plan for your dating partner? What would you do if God's purpose for you involved terminating your current relationship?

3. How compatible are your and your partner's opinions on finances, credit usage, and debt levels? What about religion and politics? Do you share similar views on size of family, child discipline, home location, frequency of family visits, and family-shared holiday visits or vacations? What about medical conditions or treatments? Do you agree on whether to be a single- or dual-income family? How similar are your views about advanced education?

4. Do you share compatible careers? Will both of your work schedules allow sufficient time together? How much dedication and priority do each of you place on your careers as compared to your relationship?

5. Do you stimulate each other intellectually? Do you challenge each other to develop and grow through reading, sharing, learning, and discussing various topics? Are either of you hesitant to fully speak your mind in order to gain the other's acceptance or approval? Do you respectfully solicit and discuss each other's opinions about topics on which you differ? Can you disagree respectfully?

CHAPTER 11

How Does That Make You Feel?

When the word *emotional* is used, it normally does not convey a positive meaning or image. It is usually meant to reference someone's uncontrolled behaviors or moodiness. Saying someone is "so emotional" indicates a sign of weakness. *Toughen up and stop getting all emotional* describes a person with sensitive or quickly changing feelings. *Don't trust your feelings—you'll feel differently tomorrow* reflects a mindset of not giving your feelings much credibility.

When you were younger, you readily expressed honest feelings. You cried when you felt pain. You hollered when you were hungry. You cooed and smiled when you were happy. You took a toy away from someone else when you felt like it.

But as you grew older, the *emotional* aspect of life became confusing and contradictory. You came to realize that emotional expressions are stereotyped by gender. Girls are conditioned to believe it's okay to cry when hurt. Boys are conditioned to believe it's never okay to cry; when hurt they must play through the pain. Girls are encouraged to express emotional authenticity; boys are encouraged to bottle everything up inside. Women are expected to be nurturing and emotional. Men are expected to be stoic and tough. It is acceptable for women to talk nonstop with their friends, hug at every possible moment, and make group trips to the restroom for more talking. It is acceptable for men to grunt one or two words to each other, fist-bump or high-five, and make solo trips to the restroom—where talking is strictly forbidden. Add to these differences the hormonal effects of estrogen and testosterone and we encounter the complex world of emotional interaction.

As you pursue a fulfilling and abundant life with a compatible partner, recognize the importance of emotional maturity and interdependence with the other three aspects of life. The *emotional* aspect involves your soul; it encompasses your feelings, intuition, and interactive experience with other people.

The Significance of Your Soul

When God breathed His breath into man, man became a "living soul" (Genesis 2:7 KJV). Various resources reveal the Hebrew and Greek definitions for *soul* as the divine breath of a living creature. Some people associate it with the spirit. However, enough distinction exists to allow for a separation between the soul and the spirit (Matthew 12:18; I Corinthians 15:45; I Thessalonians 5:23; Hebrews 4:12).

Just because a living being has the "life element" (spirit) does not necessarily mean it is aware of its surroundings. Just because something is alive does not mean it can experience emotions as a result of interaction with its surroundings. A tree has life but is not aware of what is around it. A comatose person may still be alive, yet experiences little or no emotions.

> The soul is the horizontal window that makes you aware of your environment. It allows you to feel and express emotions.

The *spirit* is the living vitality

and consciousness of God. The ~~soul~~ *soul* is the horizontal window that makes you aware of your environment.[34] The soul allows you to feel and express emotions. It is the extension of who you are and the expression of what you feel. The soul is sometimes considered synonymous with the heart. Not your physical, beating heart, but the inner core of your being.

The *emotional* aspect of life is the intangible component that gives you the capacity for a deeper life. It is much more than fickle, surface-level, in-the-moment feelings. It reveals your inner desire for connection with another person. Without emotions, you would be a robot. With no feelings, you would simply perform the obligatory actions of your daily schedule and personal interactions, but you would not truly experience or express anything.

Granted, there is a downside to emotions. Having emotional capacity creates the potential for feelings such as fear, anger, jealousy, depression, and hate. Removing the negative side of this aspect would be a favorable argument for eliminating

> We honor God by genuinely expressing and appropriately enjoying our emotions.

it altogether. But God does not intend for us to exist as robots or merely "get through this life." He wants us to experience life richly and abundantly (John 10:10). We honor God by genuinely expressing and appropriately enjoying our emotions with Him, with other people, and within the creation in which He placed us.

Emotional capacity is one of the components of being made in God's image. Many Scripture verses reference the various emotions God the Father exhibits. Love (John 3:16), hatred (Proverbs 6:16-19), anger (Numbers 11:1), jealousy (Exodus 34:14), and compassion (Psalm 86:15) are just a few.

While here on earth, Jesus, God the Son, also demonstrated a variety of emotions. As a complete and mature man, He exhibited a variety of healthy emotions including:

- Tenderness and affection with children (Mark 10:13-16)
- Meekness and gentleness of spirit (II Corinthians 10:1)
- Joy with His disciples (John 15:11)
- Humility when washing the disciples' feet (John 13:4-5)
- Grief over a friend's death (John 11:33-36)
- Reassuring peace and comfort (John 14:27-28)
- Anger toward sin (John 2:14-17)
- Love for the world (John 3:16; 15:13)

Jesus gave a great example that clarifies the genuine expression of emotions. He said a tree yields fruit according to the type of tree it is. A good tree gives good fruit. A bad tree gives bad fruit. Every tree is known by the type of fruit it gives (Luke 6:43-44). We will not find cherries on an apple tree or peaches on a grapevine. The external fruit is proof of the inner nature of the plant. The same holds true for you.

Jesus said a good man, out of the good treasure of his heart, reflects good fruit. An evil man, out of the evil treasure of his heart, exhibits evil fruit. For "out of the abundance [or overflow] of the heart his mouth speaks" (Luke 6:45 NKJV, brackets added). What is on the inside comes out. People who habitually use vulgar or harsh language generally have crude and mean-spirited sentiments at the core of their being. Similarly, those who regularly exhibit compassion, peace, purity, and love usually have a benevolent core.

What you feel inside is usually confirmed outwardly. When you are happy or content, you reflect it by a happy, peaceful expression. When you are anxious, it shows through nervous behavior or a worried look. If you are grieving, you may express it through tears or quietness.

It is possible to mask your feelings. For example, you may put on a "brave face" in a frightening situation. You may put on a "happy face" while attending a social function you would rather not attend. Sometimes the behavior does not match what is truly felt inside. If a person hosts a wild and crazy all-night party, you might find it difficult to believe that person is grieving. If a person constantly displays a depressed, gloomy expression, you may not believe that person is very happy. The same holds true for those who claim to be Spirit-filled Christians yet have no outward demonstration of spiritual "fruit."

From a relationship perspective, this disbelief applies to those who claim to love someone deeply, yet do little or nothing of meaningful value to outwardly prove that love. If a person claims to love someone, yet expresses no genuine emotional response (as opposed to obligatory action), the suspicion is that her love may not be genuine. Or even love at all! Jesus referred to this by saying that some of His professing followers talked a good game, but their hearts were far from Him (Matthew 15:8; Mark 7:6). Your emotional response generally reveals your true inner feelings.

> Your emotional response generally reveals your true inner feelings.

Emotional Interaction with the Other Three Aspects

To have an interdependent and fulfilling life, we must acknowledge, understand, and develop the *emotional* aspect as part of who we are and what we feel. While healthy, mature, and balanced emotions bring the other three aspects to life, harmful, immature, and imbalanced emotions create conflict and lead to relational problems. Emotions provide the *feeling and sensory experience* for the other three aspects.

Your emotions are interdependent with the other three aspects. Two Harvard-associated experts validate this by describing how emotions affect the spirit, mind, and body.

> *Emotions are always present and often affect your experience. You may try to ignore them, but they will not ignore you.*

*Emotions affect your body. Emotions can have an imme-
diate impact on your physiology, causing you to perspire,
to blush, to laugh, or to feel butterflies in your stomach.
After you feel an emotion, you may try to control the
expression of that emotion. But your body still experiences
physiological changes.*

*Emotions affect your thinking. When you feel disappoint-
ment or anger, your head clogs with negative thoughts.
Negative thinking crowds out space in your brain for
learning, thinking, and remembering. When you feel positive emotions, in contrast, your thoughts often center on
what is right about you, others, or ideas . . . your thinking
becomes more open, creative, and flexible.*

*Emotions affect your behavior. Virtually every emotion
you feel motivates you to take action. If you are exuberant,
you may feel a physical impulse to hug the other side. If
you are angry, you may feel like hitting them.*[35]

Your goal should be emotional behavior and expressions that
appropriately support and positively interact with your *spiritual,
intellectual,* and *physical* aspects. Left to themselves, your emotions
can lead you into deep trouble. Reverend Billy Graham shares the
following insight on this:

*Emotions in themselves aren't wrong or sinful—not at
all. God gave our emotions to us, and we shouldn't despise
or deny them. God experiences emotion—and so do we,
because we were made in his image. How empty our
lives would be if we had no emotions! Like everything
else, however, our emotions have been corrupted by sin.
Emotions aren't bad in themselves, but they can become
twisted or even destructive. Satan will try to use them to
gain victory over us. In fact, one of Satan's chief ways of
attacking us is through our emotions. Learn to guard the
"gate" of your emotions!*[36]

Spiritually, you are to protect your heart with all diligence (Proverbs 4:23 KJV). Intellectually, you are to control your thoughts and your mind (II Corinthians 10:5). Emotionally, you are to exercise the same self-discipline. If you do not control your feelings, they will control you.

> If you do not control your feelings, they will control you.

Spiritually

Without emotions, there is no meaningful worship of God. There is no genuine compassion for others. There is no true remorse and repentance when we sin. There is no real evidence of the Holy Spirit in our lives.

The *emotional* aspect provides the appropriate channel through which the evidence of the Holy Spirit may flow. Scripture says the fruit or evidence of the Spirit is love, joy, peace, patience, kindness, goodness, faithfulness, gentleness, and self-control (Galatians 5:22-23). Most of these are behavioral traits derived from positive emotions. Can you show true love without emotion? Can you demonstrate real joy without emotion? Can you display genuine peacefulness without emotional tranquility? Without emotional expression, it is difficult to exhibit the fruit of the Spirit.

The fruit of the Spirit is the evidence of the Holy Spirit's influence on your life. You demonstrate this "fruit" through genuine emotional expression. If you love out of a sense of duty and not with genuine feeling, it will not feel like love to those whom you express it. If you are kind out of obligation and not true feelings, it will not come across as kindness. The genuineness of your emotions is what makes them meaningful.

> The genuineness of your emotions is what makes them meaningful.

A mature and balanced *emotional* aspect provides the freedom for genuine emotional expression. God expresses genuine emotions and He has created you in His image to do the same. Express those emotions that come from healthy balances in the other three aspects. Align your feelings and emotional expressions with the moral framework of your *spiritual* aspect.

Intellectually

There is nothing like the feeling of being in love! But, how would you respond if someone asked you, *Why do you feel the way you do about your dating partner?* Could you readily identify practical reasons? Or would you simply describe your feelings? *She makes me happy. I feel a deep connection with him. She makes my insides turn to mush. When I look at him, I feel lightheaded and weak at the knees.*

These feelings may be real and dear to you, but it is important to engage your sound reasoning capacity. Though it may be difficult to do, step back and analyze your feelings. Ask yourself, *Are my feelings reasonable, genuine, and mutual? Or are they the result of my spiritual weakness, surface-level attraction, and/or my emotional neediness?* Then have the courage to answer honestly. Keep in mind, your heart will sometimes mislead you (Jeremiah 17:9). Since God examines both your heart and your mind (Jeremiah 17:10), make sure both are in agreement and aligned with His Word.

Physically

Romantic feelings can be so intense that they overpower your spirit and overwhelm your mind. When you are attracted to another person, your emotions affect your *physical* aspect, resulting in cold sweats, nervousness, butterflies in your stomach, and strong urges to become physically involved. If uncontrolled, such passionate feelings may lead you into actions you later regret.

In your lifetime, you will feel strongly about someone, maybe even several "someones"! These feelings are normal, but severe consequences occur if you allow them to control your relational behavior. Wait until you find "that" someone who feels as intensely as you do, with whom you are compatible and interdependent in all four aspects. An emotionally mature person will balance strong feelings with spiritual morality and intellectual reason. *Am I going to obey God and stay true to my moral convictions? Will the decision I make honor God or result in guilt and regret?*

Paul advised young Timothy to live his life as a positive example for others to follow. This included his words, his lifestyle, his loving affection, his strong faith, and his purity of conduct (I Timothy 4:12). Paul also instructed believers to stay away from the very "appearance of evil" (I Thessalonians 5:22, KJV). You control your sexual impulses by not toying with them. Don't see how physically involved you can get before stopping. God created you to experience passionate, loving feelings—but He intends for you to act on them fully only when you are married.

How the *Emotional* Aspect Affects Relationships

Emotional *dependency* occurs when we depend on someone else for our emotional well-being. We derive our sense of self-worth from that person's affirmation or by our association with him or her. This is sometimes referred to as being emotionally "needy" or "clingy." This "neediness" implies an emotional immaturity that leaves us vulnerable to the harmful and controlling actions of others. For example, when someone says he loves you, it makes you feel wonderful and whole. When that person changes his mind, you are devastated and feel worthless because your emotional well-being is dependent on him.

Emotional *interdependency* occurs when two people are emotionally mature and have a healthy sense of self-worth. They combine their emotional strengths to positively influence and support each other. In this type of interaction, there is no controlling or harmful action from either person. Their emotional expression is genuine and not manipulative. If the relationship ends, heartache may exist, but their self-worth remains intact.

An ideal mate should be a compatible match to your level of emotional maturity, intensity, freedom of expression, and needs.

When you are considering someone as a potential partner, observe that person's emotional level and intensity, then compare it to your own. An ideal mate should be a compatible match to your level of emotional maturity, intensity, freedom of expression, and needs.

An emotional romantic and a dispassionate realist will have very different emotional levels, expressions, and needs. If they were to view a sunset together, the romantic may describe it as an amazing display of stunning colors etched across the clouds. It will soon vanish from sight and there will never be another one like it. Surely, this magnificent scene was meant specifically for them on this special occasion. The romantic partner snuggles up close to the one he loves, breathes in deeply, and softly whispers sweet nothings in her ear. Ahh, can you feel it?

His companion, the realist, will point out that sunsets happen every night. She will explain that the colors are merely a reflection of light rays from the sun. And the sun does not really "set"—the earth's rotation provides the illusion of the sun setting. Speaking of which, it's getting dark, the mosquitoes are out, and there are things that must be done, so they really should be going.

The romantic will experience feelings of frustration due to his unmet expectations and may respond with mood-killing quietness. The realist will not understand the problem with stating factual observations and will wonder why she's getting the cold-shoulder treatment.

If this scenario occurs while they are dating, the romantic might tell the realist to take her logic and go find another brainiac to love. The realist would consider his reaction as a perfect example of how crazy "mushy" people can get.

The dating phase is the perfect time to discover whether emotional compatibility exists. *Prior to* committing to a more serious level in the relationship, both people should determine if their emotional differences are tolerable or deal-breakers.

In some instances, opposites can complete each other by bringing balance to the relationship. Romantics can help realists recognize the beauty around them, while realists can keep romantics grounded in the practical world. Other times, such differences can tear a relationship apart, along with both of the people in it.

It is true that opposites often attract, at least initially. We are naturally drawn to character traits we wish we had. An introvert may be attracted to an extrovert who easily socializes with everyone. However, in a dating relationship, that socializing could lead the introvert to feel jealous. An outgoing woman may be drawn to a man who is the "strong, silent type." Then in a relationship, she wonders why he doesn't talk to her more. Similarly, the "strong, silent type" may enjoy dating an outgoing woman who keeps conversations going and can discuss many interesting topics. But after a few years of marriage, he may wonder if she will ever shut up!

> *"Opposites attract" may be a common phenomenon but doesn't necessarily lead to a strong marriage. Far too often what seemed irresistible in the swirl of hormones and emotional highs during a fast courtship turns out to be irritating in the 24/7, "up close and personal" daily life of husband and wife. The mature and responsible guy seems to become a stiff, nit-picking perfectionist, boring and sexually uninteresting. The girl who appeared to be such a wonderful, bouncy, free spirit now looks like an irresponsible, immature twit with no depth at all.*[37]

More often than not, successful, long-term relationships follow the "birds of a feather flock together" concept. Similar preferences tend to fit within your comfort zone. However, that doesn't mean relationships between opposites are doomed. Just know that significant emotional differences may bring added frustration and a greater need for tolerance to the relationship.

> Without a true connection in the *emotional* aspect, you risk having a frustrated, incomplete, and unfulfilled relationship.

Without a true connection in the *emotional* aspect, you risk having a frustrated, incomplete, and unfulfilled relationship. A much better choice would be to find fulfillment through emotional compatibility that is balanced and interdependent with the other three aspects of your life. When you accurately identify and achieve emotional compatibility with another person, you truly "connect" with that person. When that connection is aligned with your moral *spirit* and supported by your rational *mind*, your relationship stands a greater chance of abundantly succeeding rather than simply existing.

Emotional Development and Maturity

Have you ever known people who were emotionally attached to partners who were harmful to them or took advantage of them? What is it that draws a woman, who is seeking acceptance and attention, to a conquest-minded man who knows just what to tell her to get what he wants from her? What makes her give herself to him emotionally and physically? What is it that attracts a man, who is lacking in self-confidence and self-worth, to a seductive, manipulative woman who knows how to act and dress to get what she wants from him? What makes him submit to such abuse? What makes people believe that harmful and disrespectful relationships are better than none at all?

The urge to be accepted by and connected with another person is strong. When your heart hears all the sweet things it wants to hear, you experience an intense desire to become physically involved with that person. One thing leads to another, and before you know it, you are having premarital sex. Too late you realize how little you have in common—yet you have already shared yourself intimately. Feelings of spiritual guilt, intellectual regret, and emotional emptiness then cause you to lower your relational expectations or make excuses for your incompatibilities with this person.

Allowing an emotional imbalance to overrule your better judgment in the other aspects leads to an unfulfilled relationship. Your focus should be to outgrow any such dependent immaturity *long before* entering into a serious relationship. The desire for connection is acceptable. Allowing it to control you is not.

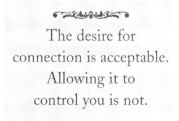

The desire for connection is acceptable. Allowing it to control you is not.

Only after you develop emotional maturity should you look for a romantic relationship. After all, how can you recognize commonalities or compatibility with someone else if your own development is immature or imbalanced?

Developing your emotional maturity before seriously dating anyone benefits you in various ways.

- *You can better understand your own emotional level, intensity, and needs.* For example, are you a romantic or realist, extrovert or introvert, shy or outgoing, quiet or loud, rebellious or compliant? The more emotionally mature you become, the more you will understand your personality and your needs, desires, and expectations in a spouse.
- *You can more readily identify and observe the emotional behaviors of other people.* Is your dating partner serious or lighthearted, moody or expressive, angry or calm, guarded or open, needy or mature, jealous or trusting? Emotional maturity makes it easier to assess your dating partner's personality and emotional characteristics and thus determine whether that person meets your emotional needs and desires.
- *You can better compare your emotional aspect to the emotional level, intensity, and needs of the people you date.* What attracts you? What frustrates you? What faults can you overlook? Instead of prematurely becoming emotionally attached and

then dealing with incompatibilities, identify any emotional disconnects early on in the relationship. Then you can decide whether you can live with or work through the differences— or terminate the relationship altogether. Either way, you've made an informed, mature choice instead of simply reacting to an imbalanced emotional desire in your life.

Signs of Emotional Maturity

Emotional maturity takes place as you gain experience from your interactions with people. Here are some ways of demonstrating growth and personal maturity in the *emotional* aspect:

- *Know who you are.* Instead of just living your life experiences, stop and consider your responses to those experiences. When you feel impatience with other drivers, fondness for romance novels, angry outbursts when confronted, or compassion for your disabled neighbor, ask yourself why you responded as you did. Make a list of your emotional strengths and weaknesses. As you interact with people, make note of your feelings regarding different situations. Take a personality test, a spiritual gifts test, or any other reputable questionnaire to help you understand who you are. Experiences like these help put your life's "puzzle" together and give you insight as to who you are.
- *Observe the emotional interactions of others.* Start with your immediate and extended family members. Analyze their emotional makeup and intensity. You are a part of their gene pool and may share quite a few emotional tendencies. During group social functions, instead of getting caught up in the festivities and sensations, observe the behaviors, interactions, and intensity levels of others. A person may be nice on the surface, but not truly compassionate. Polite, but not truly respectful. Likeable, but not truly loveable. Make note of which responses attract you and which do not.
- *Control your emotions.* Emotional maturity occurs when control over your emotions shifts from your parents or other authority figures to you. When you were a child and did not get

your way, you responded in an emotionally uncontrolled manner. But as you mature, you put away such childish responses (I Corinthians 13:11). Learn when and how to express your feelings as well as when and how to restrain yourself.

- *Be comfortable experiencing and sharing heartfelt emotions.* Be strong enough to shed a tear. Tough enough to be tender. Confident enough to be humble. Secure enough to be vulnerable. Honest enough to be real. Bold enough to be respectful. Courageous enough to experience, express, and enjoy all the healthy emotions God wants you to experience.

- *Move past dependence and independence into interdependence.* In emotional interdependence, both people are sensitive to each other's emotional needs and support each other while not depending on each other for their self-worth. Guard against any harmful and premature attachments as well as any self-centered arrogance. Develop the emotional strength to be patient and wait for someone who meets all (not just most) of your expectations and who is compatible in all (not just some) aspects.

Emotional Compatibility Questionnaire

Here are a few questions to consider when determining the emotional expectations you have for a potential spouse. Use it as a starting point to create your own list of questions. The answers will help initiate the process of discovering emotional compatibility in a relationship. Keep in mind that emotional compatibility involves the *number* of desired emotional behaviors and traits as well as the *quality* of emotional depth and connection.

1. Do you always fully enjoy each other's company, or are there times when you are concerned about your dating partner's embarrassing behavior or unusual traits? Can you accept and live with these traits or are they deal breakers?
2. Do you share a compatible level of respect for each other, your parents, and your friends? What have you learned about your dating partner's emotional capacity while observing his or

her emotional interaction with parents, family, and friends? How do you each interact emotionally with others around you (siblings, friends, waiters, children, other drivers on the road, authority figures, etc.)?

3. How do you demonstrate your emotional support for each other? Does your dating partner pick up on your emotional state, or must you initiate a discussion to draw attention to it? Are you both in tune with each other's emotional well-being? Would you rate your relationship as *dependent*, *independent*, or *interdependent*?

4. Can you openly and honestly share your feelings and thoughts with your partner without fear, shame, competition, or rejection? Or must you hint, drop subtle clues, or play "twenty questions" to arrive at the topic of choice?

5. How do you demonstrate your emotional connection to each other? Are you comfortable just *being* together, without having to *do* anything? Or does your relationship consist of going from one social activity or event to another without any downtime?

6. When you observe a beautiful sunset, do you share a similar appreciation? How about an emotional or romantic movie? Do you consider a walk on the beach at night an opportunity for exercise, a precursor to sexual activity, or a time of emotional connection?

CHAPTER 12

Takin' Care of Your Clay

He placed one scoop of clay upon another until a form lay lifeless on the ground.

The Maker looked earnestly at the clay creation. A monsoon of love swelled up within him. He had died for the creation before he had made him. God's form bent over the sculptured face and breathed. Dust stirred on the lips of the new one. The chest rose, cracking the red mud. The cheeks fleshened. A finger moved. And an eye opened.[38]

Your body is the temporary physical address where your spirit, mind, and soul reside. With the body, God gives you the ability to physically interact with and experience His creation. You use your body in your worship of God, your service to God, and your physical interaction with other people. From a relationship perspective, the *physical* aspect involves all bodily contact and interaction, physical affection, and sexual intimacy.

Your tangible body enables your intangible spirit, mind, and soul to express themselves and experience life. When you see a majestic mountain landscape, the *physical* aspect gives you the

> The *physical* aspect expresses the *spiritual, intellectual,* and *emotional* aspects.

channel through which to capture the awe-inspiring view. You use your body to travel to the site and walk among the trees. You smell the scent of pine in the air. See the magnificent beauty. Hear the leaves rustling in the wind. Feel the trail beneath your feet. Your *spirit* praises the Creator for His marvelous works. Your *mind* acknowledges the precision of His handiwork. Your *soul* experiences and thrives on the beauty of His creation. The *physical* aspect expresses the *spiritual, intellectual,* and *emotional* aspects— it is the embodiment of the spirit, mind, and soul.

In a marriage ceremony, the minister or public official does *not* say, "You may kiss the bride's spirit, mind, or emotions." Rather, "You may kiss the bride." The shared physical kiss is the symbolic expression of the mutual feelings and commitment of the relationship. Your body is the enabler of your feelings of love, affection, and desire.

The Significance of Your Body

As with the other three aspects, the *physical* holds the potential for both good and evil. We activate that opposing potential with the choices we make.

- The same hand that softly caresses can also painfully strike.
- The same mouth that sings praises can also spew hatred.
- The same eyes that behold beauty can also look lustfully.
- The same ears that hear God's call can also heed sin's seduction.
- The same feet that lead a person to church can also lead him astray.

Some people believe you can act as you wish since you own your body. But the reality is that you do not. When you were born, you had no choice of the type of body you received. You can eat healthy but still get sick. You can exercise, but you will still die.

The only part that you "own" is the personal accountability for your choices in how you use the body God gave you. It is not yours; it belongs to God and He wants you to use it to honor Him (I Corinthians 6:19-20).

Depending on your choices, you will experience either positive rewards or negative consequences. When you choose positive behaviors, you experience rewards. For example, if you choose a healthy diet and lifestyle consisting of regular exercise, your body will reward you with strength and energy. If you choose to be sexually chaste in your conduct before marriage, you honor God and will receive His blessing. You also avoid the anxiety, embarrassment, and loss of innocence brought on by an unwed pregnancy, a sexually transmitted disease, or betrayal of trust.

However, if you do not exercise balance and self-control in the *physical* aspect, great harm can occur. Every day there are news stories of murders, violence, drug abuse, and sexual misconduct involving political, religious, and community leaders. You may even have your own sordid stories. Lives are devastated. Future plans forever changed. Families torn apart. Careers destroyed. Reputations ruined. Respect lost.

> If you do not exercise balance and self-control in the *physical* aspect, great harm can occur.

James explains the destructive process that occurs when you allow your physical desires to overrule your spirit, mind, and soul. "Temptation comes from our own desires, which entice us and drag us away. These desires give birth to sinful actions. And when sin is allowed to grow, it gives birth to death" (James 1:14-15 NLT). When you allow harmful actions to move unrestrained through your life, those actions negatively affect your entire being.

For example, the sin of lust starts with an uncontrolled desire, moves to a lingering look, then becomes a prolonged thought in the *mind*. It proceeds to an overruled conviction in the *spirit,* then degenerates to an enflamed arousal of the *emotions*. If not controlled, it produces a sinful physical action. The same progression applies to any sinful deed, including slander, gossip, rebellion, theft, and even murder.

Physical vulnerability and temptation are not only the result of poor choices or lack of self-control. We also have an enemy who is always in full attack mode. When the serpent targeted Eve in the Garden of Eden, he presented her with something that was physically appealing. She failed to recognize it as an assault meant to destroy her. Satan attacks us with the same devious plan. He tempts us with things or situations that have a strong physical appeal.

If he can influence you to compromise your spiritual morals, he can cripple you with guilt. If he can lure you into immoral decisions, he can defeat you with self-doubt and regret. If he can get you to yield to carnal feelings, he can enslave you with sexual addiction. If he can get you to stumble and fall due to an imbalanced or uncontrolled *physical* aspect, he knows he can cause you irreparable harm.

For this reason, God gives this warning: "Be self-controlled and alert. Your enemy the devil prowls around like a roaring lion looking for someone to devour" (I Peter 5:8). Satan is aggressively looking for ways to overwhelm and destroy you.

> Every person has a specific sinful vulnerability.

To protect against Satan's attack, God's instruction is to "put on the full armor of God so that you can take your stand against the devil's schemes" (Ephesians 6:11). You cannot protect yourself strictly through self-discipline. You must apply God's Word to every aspect of your life. God also counsels us to "throw off everything that hinders and the sin that so easily entangles" (Hebrews 12:1). Notice the singular phrase *the sin* in this verse. Every person has a specific sinful vulnerability. It is your "pet sin" against which you must always be on guard.

You cannot approach immoral behavior with a lighthearted attitude. Solomon warns, "Can a man scoop fire into his lap without his clothes being burned?" (Proverbs 6:27). The danger of being burned is the reason you don't play with fire. Sin's devastating consequences are why you must not experiment or casually toy with sinful activities. No matter the peer pressure. Regardless of who else is doing it. In spite of your passionate feelings at the moment.

Physical Interaction with the Other Three Aspects

Of all the four aspects, the *physical* most desperately needs the interaction and balance of the others. Our inherent sinful nature craves sinful thoughts and actions. However, Paul warns us to not let sinful habits control our bodies (Romans 6:12). You must protect your spirit, your thoughts (mind), and your soul (emotions). The body requires the same high level of protection. You accomplish this protection through the interdependence of all four aspects of life.

Before you act:

- Filter your actions through God's Word and the morality of the *spiritual* aspect.
- Analyze your actions through the reasoning of the *intellectual* aspect; then align your actions with godly values.
- Examine the feelings and desires that are prompting your actions with the genuineness and appropriateness of the *emotional* aspect; then allow only those feelings and actions that are supported by spiritual and intellectual input.

The *physical* aspect by itself is quite hollow. When you overemphasize it and separate it from the other three aspects, you create an unhealthy imbalance in your life. Yes, the *physical* can offer immediate attraction, instant pleasure, and sexual gratifica-

> The *physical* aspect by itself is quite hollow.

tion. However, it provides lasting fulfillment and satisfaction only when it occurs within marriage and is interdependent with the other three aspects.

Spiritually

> When you engage in sexual activity prior to marriage, you are taking something that is not yours.

A mature and balanced *physical* aspect acts within the moral restraint of the *spiritual* aspect. Before marriage, physical affection must not lead to sexual activity. It is God's desire that all sexual activity take place within marriage (I Thessalonians 4:3). This includes all sexual fondling, oral sex, and sexual intercourse. What you learned as a child ("Keep your hands to yourself") still applies when you are grown. When you engage in sexual activity prior to marriage, you are taking something that is not yours. Even if someone seductively offers you sexual activity, refuse. Prior to marriage, it is not yours to take and it is not his or hers to give.

Think about your account at your financial institution. Another person cannot legally access your funds unless his name is on the account. Only by you adding his name on the account is he able to gain access to the funds. The same restriction should be in place regarding your sexual purity. No matter how passionately you feel about another person, no one should gain access to your body unless he has "legal access" to it. In God's eyes, that legal access is marriage. When you engage in sexual immorality, you sin against your own body (I Corinthians 6:18) and against God (Psalm 51:4).

Within marriage, however, God intends for a couple's physical union to be one of mutual enjoyment and pleasure. Along with an entire book devoted to it (Song of Solomon), Scripture contains many references to the happiness (Isaiah 62:5; Psalm 19:5), affection (I Corinthians 7:3), honor (Hebrews 13:4), respect (I Peter

3:7), and sheer enjoyment (Proverbs 5:18-19; Song of Solomon) of physical involvement after marriage.

Intellectually

Mature people allow only those behaviors that are governed by sound reason and moral restraint. Peter, who was known to act and speak irrationally at times, shares the secret he learned about controlling our actions. "Be alert and think straight. Don't let your lives be controlled by your desires. Always live as God's holy people should" (I Peter 1:13-16, CEV).

> Mature people allow only those behaviors that are governed by sound reason and moral restraint.

Paul advised Timothy to teach young men and women to be "sober minded" (Titus 2:4, 6). This means to be self-controlled regarding your passions. Use your mind and spirit to control the emotional impulses and physical urges you may experience prior to marriage.

King David learned the hard way the value of making wise choices when he had his encounter with Bathsheba (II Samuel 11:2-27). While walking along his rooftop one evening, he saw his attractive neighbor as she was bathing. Instead of making the smart and honorable choice to turn away, he continued watching. Then he started asking other people about her. Ignoring the fact she was married, he invited her to his palace and ultimately had sex with her. That sin led to other sins, including the murder of her husband. The steep price David paid for his sin included several deaths in his family and challenges to his kingdom. But he learned a valuable lesson from it. He wrote, "I will be careful to live a blameless life. I will lead a life of integrity in my own home. I will refuse to look at anything vile and vulgar" (Psalm 101:2-3, NLT). David learned, through deep sorrow and lifelong regret, that living a pure life involved refusing to look upon any lustful sights and guarding against them from entering his mind.

Each day, we face situations that require a moral choice. With the prevalence of sexual and pornographic images everywhere (magazines, movies, the Internet, etc.), we must choose to refuse the entrance of such immoral garbage into our lives. A sound mind that is governed by the morality of a mature and balanced *spiritual* aspect will help you live a pure life and make choices that honor God.

Emotionally

A strong level of trust and self-control is required when two people approach the physical stage of their relationship. Due to its powerful attraction, involvement at this level should take place *only after* proper progression through the other three aspects. First, you must be a compatible match spiritually and intellectually. This is where you determine if you *like* someone. Then a compatible emotional connection may occur. This is where you decide whether you *love* someone. The *physical* aspect is the final stage in a relationship. Mutually compatible levels in each aspect should be determined before moving to the next.

If you have no common ground spiritually with someone, then looking for shared intellectual levels is pointless. If there is no compatibility spiritually and intellectually, then becoming emotionally attached is foolish. Finally, unless you are compatible in spirit, mind, and soul, you should not get involved physically or consider marriage with that person.

Do not risk long-term satisfaction by physically "experimenting" during courtship. Peter urges us to "abstain from the sensual urges (evil desires; passions of the flesh) that wage war against the soul" (I Peter 2:11, AMP). Do not sacrifice lifelong fulfillment by surrendering to immediate, passionate, and uncontrolled feelings that lead to premarital sex. Keep in mind:

*You can generally do something you have
not yet done, but anticipate doing;*

*But you can never undo something you
have already done and regret.*

How the *Physical* Aspect Affects Relationships

Achieving and participating in the *physical* aspect of a relationship does not make the other aspects unnecessary or less critical. A physical relationship without spiritual values, intellectual respect, and emotional connection is unsatisfactory and unfulfilling. It is the equivalent of trying to have a conversation with someone who is not truly paying attention. She may be there bodily, but not mentally or emotionally, and the conversation suffers.

Sexual involvement without the support and interdependence of the other aspects results in unexpressed feelings or unfulfilled expectations. Such physical relationships are generally short-term, strained, and unsatisfactory. They also run a high risk of failure.

The *physical* aspect requires as much compatibility as the other three aspects. Physical commonalities include attraction and chemistry, levels of affection, comfort with public displays of affection, and expectations regarding sexual intimacy.

> The *physical* aspect requires as much compatibility as the other three aspects.

Sexual incompatibility is one of the main reasons for unsatisfied marriages, infidelity, and divorce.[39] Many things can contribute to sexual incompatibility. Obsession with marriage. Overlooking key differences in relational expectations. Marrying for the wrong reasons. Weak chemistry. Lack of understanding of the importance of sex. Poor communication related to sexual expectations.

Historically, the church has considered sex as carnal, sinful, and a spiritual hindrance. When not presented as such, church teaching has been relatively silent regarding the pleasure God intends for sex to bring to a marriage.

Throughout Christian history, people have been taught

that sexuality is bad, or at best, a necessary evil. St. Augustine believed that the less one was driven toward sex, and the less pleasure he received from it, the more sure he could be of his sanctification. St. Thomas Aquinas believed that the sexual act was only for procreation. If intercourse was engaged in for any other reason, it was sin. It was not until Martin Luther declared, "We are justified by faith," that Christians began to realize other dimensions of our sexual nature. Sexuality is part of our God-given nature. Sexuality, then, is not only a physical drive...but it involves the whole being of man. Thus, sexuality is a good gift from God. God created and intended it for pleasure, not indiscriminate use.[40]

What effect has this distorted view of physical intimacy had on the church? Compared to the national average divorce rate of approximately 50 percent, the statistics for conservative Christians are not much better. The divorce rates by religious group are: nondenominational Christians (34 percent), Baptists (29 percent), and mainline Protestants (25 percent).[41] Though lower than the national average, the high number of divorces for Christians is still discouraging and embarrassing.

By simply quoting "husbands, love your wives," "wives, be submissive to your husbands," and "God hates divorce," churches perpetuate relational problems. Instead of downplaying or ignoring emotional feelings and physical pleasures, they should offer sound biblical guidance that includes all four aspects. They should remind everyone that God gives us all things to abundantly enjoy (I Timothy 6:17, NKJV).

If marital sex is presented as a wife's submissive "meeting of needs," the resulting emotional disconnect leaves both spouses unfulfilled. This subservient mindset promotes selfish motives or a "checklist" mentality. If there is no sexual celebration or mutual enjoyment, the concept of marriage is reduced to nothing more than co-ed roommates who periodically exchange sexual favors.

When a couple approaches marriage from a mature and balanced four-aspect perspective, their physical union moves beyond the obligatory concept of meeting needs and into the realm of mutually enjoyable intimacy and perpetual romance.

> If there is no sexual celebration or mutual enjoyment, the concept of marriage is reduced to nothing more than co-ed roommates who periodically exchange sexual favors.

Some people think perpetual romance exists only in Fantasy Land. Why is this considered a fantasy? Is it because so few people experience it? Because so many couples settle for less? Because it is not valued, so it is allowed to fade over time? Or is it because people pursue their own selfish interests instead of being relationally interdependent? There are many reasons why people don't experience perpetual romance, but don't presume it's a fantasy simply because less-than-ideal choices have resulted in less-than-ideal relationships.

A wholesome relational approach involves all four aspects, with the body viewed not simply as a tool for sex but as an expression of the spirit, mind, and soul.

Romantic love is also elusive because most relationships are based on a union of only one or two levels or dimensions of your being. But you have four dimensions: physical, emotional, mental, and spiritual. Most relationships are based on a purely physical level, which fade with age and diminishing sexual energy. It's not that sexual attraction isn't good—it's just very incomplete—involving only a small part of your whole being. Some relationships include a union on the emotional as well as the physical level, and fewer still include the mental or intellectual level. Wholeness in a relationship results from union on all four levels.[42]

Physical Development and Maturity

> An abundant life requires balanced attention, development, and commitment in all four aspects.

An abundant life requires balanced attention, development, and commitment in all four aspects. You demonstrate maturity and wisdom when you protect yourself against anything that would restrict or harm your physical well-being. Along with nourishing and protecting your spirit, mind, and soul, also maintain healthy habits and avoid anything that is harmful to your body.

The pressures of life, ever-increasing age, and the pull of gravity all have unforgiving effects on your body. The graying or receding hairline. Wrinkles and varicose veins. Muscles that lose their youthful shape and tone. Declining stamina. They are all part of life. However, this doesn't release you from your accountability for the condition, health, and appearance of the body God gave you.

When a couple is dating, they both try to look their best. They take care of their bodies, comb their hair, separate their unibrows, shave, exercise, use deodorant and perfume/cologne, watch their diet, and maintain what they believe is at least close to their ideal weight. They each make themselves attractive and appealing to the other person. They are on their best behavior.

Yet once marriage vows are exchanged and a short period of time passes, a strange transformation seems to take place. Razor stubble shows up. Cosmetics spend more time in cabinets than on faces. The phenomenal physique that was built in the gym surrenders to the stress and fatigue of life. Fashionable weekday work clothes give way to baggy athletic wear on the weekends. Chores, mundane activities, and other priorities demand attention. Physical fitness and appearance are unintentionally placed on the back burner. The couple forgets to consider how they appear to each other. Now, this may be a matter of relaxing and getting comfortable. Or it could be a sign of taking the relationship or the other person for granted.

Preparation for marriage should include both partners committing to making themselves attractive to each other on a daily basis. This is not to say you should wear your best formalwear every day. Or that you can never have any downtime to be comfortable in your home. Just remember to take a long, hard look at what your spouse will see every day.

> Take a long, hard look at what your spouse will see every day.

Each person should respect himself (and his spouse) enough to do what is necessary to maintain a high level of appeal for each other. This is not an encouragement for cosmetic surgical enhancements. It is a reminder to take care of your body the way you do your spirit, mind, and soul.

Perpetual romance involves an ongoing effort to stay physically attractive and in overall good health. It also provides the opportunity to engage in fitness-friendly activities that are mutually enjoyable. Such activities include taking walks together, exercising at the gym together, and maintaining healthy eating habits. Even enjoying more frequent sex has health benefits. Married couples who have frequent sex tend to live longer and have healthier hearts, lower rates of certain cancers, and slimmer physiques.[43]

Never forget that Satan is actively seeking to destroy you. He attacks anyone and anything that is lovely, useful, or God-ordained (I Peter 5:8). Ever since God established the institutions of marriage and the family, the devil has been trying to break them apart. He does not limit his assault to just the *spiritual* aspect. He also attacks the mind, emotions, and body. If he can derail you from your life's purpose through a clouded mind, unstable emotions, or poor physical health, he will. If he can influence you to disregard or misuse your body so you become physically unfit, he will. He will also use your lack of attention to physical health to make you vulnerable to various temptations and harmful situations.

For example, if a husband becomes physically unfit, gains weight, and loses any desire for physical activity, he creates an unhealthy situation for himself. He also opens the door for his wife to be tempted as she interacts with her male coworkers who are physically fit and appealing. If a wife shows no interest in going to the gym with her husband, choosing rather to stay home and sit on the couch watching television, her inactivity increases her health risk. She also leaves her husband vulnerable to temptation from the spandex-clad "hotties" at the gym or from online pornography. Both spouses should actively encourage each other to participate in healthy activities they can enjoy together.

> To disregard your physical well-being and appearance is to become susceptible to more than just poor health.

Jesus reminds us of the natural temptation to point an accusing finger at the faults of others while ignoring or downplaying our own (Matthew 7:3-5). It is easy to judge those who have not exercised *moral* restraint. But we fail to point the same accusing finger at our own lack of *dietary* discipline or *wellness* self-control. To disregard your physical well-being and appearance is to become susceptible to more than just poor health.

A couple's mutual expectation of marriage should be to share a long and enjoyable lifetime together. Anything that negatively affects their physical health reduces their amount of enjoyment and the length of their lifetime together. They should avoid poor habits and addictions that contribute to poor health and encourage each other's physical well-being. Even if that means persuading each other to get off the couch and onto the treadmill, or out of the house and into the gym.

God gave you only one body. Make sure it stays in peak shape and performance for many years. As plans are made for marriage, create mutual expectations to grow old together gracefully. Commit to doing everything possible to delay the aging process and enjoying each other fully over a long and healthy lifetime together.

Signs of Physical Maturity

You may wonder why there is so much advice against getting physically involved until you are married. *Are people trying to hold me back from having fun or fully experiencing life?* Actually, the opposite is true. They are protecting and preparing you so you *can* fully experience and enjoy life upon reaching your full maturity.

Consider this illustration. If you were about to board an airline to take a flight, and you discovered that a three-year-old girl was the assigned pilot, you would probably decide to take another flight. Because of her immaturity, she does not have the capacity to safely pilot a plane. Though excited and eager to fly, she does not recognize the risks involved, nor is she trained and prepared for the task. The child is not mature enough for the experience; to allow her to proceed would be disastrous for herself and others.

Maturity involves more than reaching a certain age or physical stature. It also requires a mature spirit, mind, and soul. Here are some ways you reveal your maturity in the *physical* aspect:

- *Show respect.* This includes self-respect as well as respect for others. Move beyond being self-centered and controlled by your impulses and desires. Treat yourself and others with dignity and integrity. Be honorable in all your behavior, especially your dating behavior. Expect this behavior in your partner as well. If a dating partner does not respect you or your moral standards, then respect yourself enough to move on to someone who does.
- *Say no to yourself.* Control your desires and impulsive behaviors before they control you. If you are tempted to lie, make yourself tell the truth. If you are tempted to sneak out of the house against your parents' orders, stop yourself. If you are tempted

to engage in premarital sexual behavior, make up your mind beforehand that you will not do so. Develop the mindset to "resist the devil and he will flee from you" (James 4:7).

- *Exhibit personal accountability to a godly moral standard.* Control your actions through the morality of your *spiritual* aspect and God's Word. Appreciating physical beauty is one thing; allowing it to influence you, or viewing it as the only factor when considering a potential spouse, is a problem. Solomon's instruction is to "not lust in your heart after her beauty or let her captivate you with her eyes" (Proverbs 6:25). Keep the *physical* aspect in balance with the other three aspects.

- *Do not place yourself in vulnerable situations.* Don't make it easy for Satan to cause you to fail. Inviting your dating partner to your house when you're there alone is not wise. A weekend getaway with just you and your dating partner is risking your moral resolve. Even if nothing inappropriate happens, your reputation will be tarnished when word gets out. Stay away from even the appearance of evil (I Thessalonians 5:22). This protects you from the slippery slope of temptation. It also protects your reputation.

- *Commit to physical health and well-being.* Take care of the body God gave you. Maintain a healthy diet. Join a gym or a cycling team. Take an aerobics or yoga class. Plan a mountain hiking/ biking vacation. Commit to staying active, eating healthy, getting periodic medical exams, and maintaining overall physical wellness.

Physical Compatibility Questionnaire

Here are a few questions to consider when determining your physical expectations and compatibility in a potential spouse. Use it as a starting point to create your own list of questions. The answers will help initiate the process of discovering physical compatibility in a relationship.

1. What evidence of physical compatibility is demonstrated in your relationship? Have you remained pure in your physi-

cal involvement? Do you both agree on what behavior is and is not allowed while dating? Do your dating behaviors align with God's moral standard?

2. Has the progression through the first three aspects been mostly one-sided? Or is it a healthy reflection of how you *both* feel inwardly and are willing to express outwardly? Do either of you hold back honest feelings for fear of being rejected or worry over hurting the other person?

3. Is there a pattern of mutual attention, affection, and affirmation that is consistent with perpetual romance? Or are you simply going through the "courtship rituals" of dating?

4. Are you both comfortable with your own sexuality? Have you discussed your interest level, expectations, and needs regarding the frequency, intensity, passion level, and expression of sexual activity and intimacy? Is this an uncomfortable topic of discussion for either of you? Does it seem inappropriate due to embarrassment, immaturity, differing expectations, or lack of an established emotional safe zone?

5. Do you share compatible views regarding your enjoyment of physical contact and affection (including touching and kissing in private as well as in public)? How would you rate your anticipated enjoyment of sex?

6. How comparable are your views on when to start a family, the number of children to have, birth control measures, childbirth methods, maternity leave, etc.?

CHAPTER 13

Applying All 4 Aspects to Life

To confirm the validity and effect of the four aspects, they should make sense when we apply them to everyday life. Based on what we've learned so far, consider the following relational situations from an interdependent, four-aspect perspective. As you do, keep in mind that a fulfilling relationship involves finding a person with whom you are compatible spiritually, intellectually, emotionally, and physically.

Relational Situation #1: *I am physically involved with my boyfriend, but there is no emotional connection. Will my physical involvement create this emotional connection and eventually lead to a fulfilling relationship?*

People give many reasons for getting physically involved without a shared emotional connection. They are caught up in the passion of an uncontrolled moment. They feel obligated to "put out" because their partner expects them to. They do not want to hurt the other person's feelings. They view physical involvement as a sense of self-affirmation. They use sex as a way of controlling the relationship. They have low moral standards. The list goes on and on.

> Without the full interaction of all four aspects, sexual involvement produces emptiness, regret, depression, low self-esteem, and guilt.

Having sex can be thrilling and pleasurable—even outside of marriage. However, without emotional support, the thrill is temporary and the pleasure may not be mutually enjoyable. Without the full interaction of all four aspects, sexual involvement produces emptiness, regret, depression, low self-esteem, and guilt.[44] The Holy Spirit produces conviction in your spirit. Sound reasoning brings guilt and regret to your mind. The lack of an emotional connection creates emptiness in your soul.

Even after marriage, sexual activity merely as an obligation of the relationship is not satisfying or fulfilling. After "the deed" is done, one or both spouses experience emptiness, frustration, and/or guilt. These responses are usually triggered by the lack of an emotional connection.

Expecting fulfillment from the *physical* aspect without the full involvement and agreement of the other three aspects is like putting all the individual ingredients for a cake into a heated oven, waiting for a period of time, and expecting a cake to come out. No matter how long those separate ingredients stay in the oven, unless they are mixed together properly, they will never become a cake. Similarly, no matter how long two people are involved sexually, without the appropriate interdependence with all the other aspects, they won't have a truly fulfilling relationship.

Relational Situation #2: *For us to be emotionally compatible, my girlfriend believes I must "learn" what emotional responses she expects. Why should I have to respond in a way that I genuinely do not feel?*

Did you need to *learn* how to cry or to feel angry or content? No. These are normal, authentic emotional responses to what is taking place in the moment. Yes, it is possible to learn loving and compatible *actions* or *behaviors* based on what others expect.

But not heartfelt *feelings* that are genuinely felt, fully shared, and mutually enjoyed.

As you mature in each aspect, you develop and determine your likes and dislikes as well as your preferences and tolerances. When you watch a movie or try a new style of food, you know whether you like it or not. As an adult, you may develop a taste for something, or learn to appreciate new experiences. You may even learn to *tolerate* a few things you don't care for. But there is a vast difference between tolerating something and genuinely enjoying it.

Intimate and loving emotions shouldn't have to be learned. They should be genuinely and spontaneously felt. If emotions could be pre-programmed or premeditated, we wouldn't truly experience them or fully enjoy them.

By treating emotion as something you can learn, you overlay the *emotional* aspect with the logic of the *intellectual*. This results in an imbalance in the four aspects. Your emotions are part of who you are. You should express them naturally through genuine action or interaction. Without true emotions, you are just going through the motions.

> Without true emotions, you are just going through the motions.

Truly felt emotions, not learned behavior, prompt you to spontaneously hold your partner's face in your hands while looking deeply into her eyes, gently caressing her cheeks, and affirming your love and affection—all without having to be asked or told how. It is a natural outer expression of what is felt inside. If you have to learn how to lovingly respond and interact, your relationship must not have much emotional depth or connection. This is a main reason why purely physical relationships are short-lived. And why some marriages are shallow or strained. There is no emotional depth or connection to sustain the relationship.

Everyone deserves to be genuinely loved. Completely, passion-

> Passion is what keeps apathy and complacency from creeping in and stealing the expression and enjoyment from the relationship.

ately, and emotionally. Your emotions are God-given to be fully shared and enjoyed within the interdependence of all four aspects. There is no need to accept passive, prepro- grammed, mediocre feelings. You should be genuinely pas- sionate about the love of your life! Passion is what keeps apathy and complacency from creeping in and stealing the expression and enjoyment from the relationship.

Everyone should find someone with whom he shares a mutually passionate level. Not just physically, but in all four aspects. Find someone with whom you share genuine (not learned) emotional compatibility. If your dating partner is emotionally "unavailable" or immature, you owe it to yourself to move on. Never settle for less than complete emotional connection and the mutual celebra- tion of genuine and spontaneous feelings.

Relational Situation #3: *My girlfriend is trying to get me to fall in love by doing loving things for me. Is it possible to act our way into that feeling?*

> If an emotion must be "acted out" to be felt, it must not be real.

If an emotion must be "acted out" to be felt, it must not be real. What you feel inside—what you are truly passionate about—gen- erally comes out. Most often, you *feel* your way into an *action* (gen- uinely loving someone leads to loving action). Very seldom do you *act* your way into a genuine *feeling* (performing loving actions doesn't lead to genuine romantic love). If it were possible to act our way into a feeling, many people would *act* like millionaires! The truth is, regardless of how much they *act* rich, the balance in their checkbooks will not increase.

You can *act* as if you love someone and *do* all sorts of loving things for that person. But those actions usually do not produce genuine *feelings* of love. If, however, you feel passionately about someone, your *emotions* will generally lead to *actions*.

If your loving actions do not come from authentic emotions, how can they be considered genuine or meaningful? No one wants to receive obligatory actions. Learn to recognize the difference between heartfelt emotions and learned or "acted out" responses. As C.S. Lewis says, "You cannot feel fond of a person by trying."[45]

Relational Situation #4: *My boyfriend says he struggles with putting what he feels into words or actions. What does that mean?*

Sharing things you feel passionate about should not be difficult. Yet some people struggle with putting their emotions into words or actions. Sometimes this is the result of not having well-developed communication skills. Other times this may be due to nerves, being afraid of an embarrassing outcome, or not fully trusting their partners. But consider this: how can a person get all excited and talkative at a sporting event, yet struggle to discuss their feelings with the love of his life? People who love the beach have no problem describing it to others. Mountain bikers are not afraid to get chatty about their extreme rides. Parents who are fanatical about their kids do not struggle for words when talking about them.

It is easy and natural to talk about your subject of passion, whether it is football games, going to the spa, riding Harley motorcycles, mall shopping, hunting, amusement parks, or computer games. However, when you are not interested in or passionate about something, that is usually when you have nothing meaningful to share.

If love is genuinely felt inside, there will be acceptable evidence outside. True feelings will come out—some way, somehow.

> If love is genuinely felt inside, there will be acceptable evidence outside.

If you struggle with expressing and demonstrating genuine, spontaneous love for someone, it is highly possible there is little (if any) true feelings or connection between you and that person.

People can only express what they feel in a meaningful way, without hesitancy or fear of being vulnerable, if two requirements are met. First, what they feel must be genuine. Second, the safety and security of a relationship must be established. This usually happens during the progression through the *spiritual* and *intellectual* aspects.

Before a relationship involves your emotions, trust and honesty should exist. During the discovery of spiritual and intellectual commonalities, a "safe zone" should develop. Within this safe zone you build trust with your partner before sharing your genuine feelings. Mutual honesty and trust then enables each person to fully and freely share their true feelings.

If that safe zone does not exist, it is wise to withdraw emotionally until you identify, discuss, and resolve whatever is hindering it. There is no benefit to continue making yourself emotionally available and vulnerable if you're having trust and honesty issues. If you retreat to the sound reasoning of the *intellectual* aspect, you may discover the relationship cannot grow beyond that level.

If feelings are genuine and mutual, there should be no doubt or fear in expressing them. "There is no fear in love. But perfect [complete, fulfilled] love drives out fear" (I John 4:18, brackets added). If you find that the feelings are one-sided or not genuine, staying in the relationship is unfair to you and dishonest to your partner. Ending the relationship may be painful, but not as painful as continuing on with distrust, dishonesty, and an emotional void.

Relational Situation #5: *I've heard that the strong romantic feelings I have shouldn't be trusted since they will fade over time—it is commitment that lasts for a lifetime. Why can't I have both?*

Who says romantic feelings have to fade? If they were genuine and fully enjoyed initially, why would two people allow them to weaken? When properly nurtured, feelings can grow deeper over time. But they should never be allowed to fade. Feelings of true emotional connection are too valuable to take for granted.

> Feelings of true emotional connection are too valuable to take for granted.

If feelings do fade away, either they were not genuine to begin with, they were programmed somewhere along the way, or they were not valued enough to protect them against time's erosion.

Far too often the marriage "I do" is soon followed by a daily existence of blasé, surface-level interaction. But it doesn't *have* to be. An emotionally detached, unromantic existence is not what God intends for a married couple. As you prepare for marriage, set the expectation that both of you will actively pursue and protect your intimate feelings for each other. Determine now to create and prioritize a perpetually romantic environment in your marriage. Then, when you are married, sustain it daily with spontaneous and flirtatious actions. These actions can include:[46]

- Creating a secret sign for "I love you" or "You are adorable," then using it when you're out in public or at social gatherings.
- Holding hands whenever possible—while in the car, when taking a walk, or when riding the subway.
- Flirting with each other. Lovingly pinch each other's butt, give unexpected kisses on the lips, compliment each other, send a text or leave a voice message in the middle of the day describing your plans for later that night when you are alone together.
- Breaking out the candles—schedule one dinner a week by candlelight.
- Grinning at each other playfully as you both perform household chores.

- Bragging about each other to your friends and family—in each other's presence.
- Making one night a week movie night, with plenty of cuddling and snuggling.

Many elderly couples confirm the concept of compatible, perpetual romance. They share their attraction, affection, and affirmation throughout their lives. They stay in tune with their feelings for each other. They freely and fully share and show those feelings in a meaningful way on a daily basis. They prioritize and protect their relationship above all else.

Romantic feelings are meant to last much longer than the dating phase and the first few years of marriage. They are meant to be enjoyed for a lifetime in the affectionate environment of perpetual romance. Commit yourself to saying and doing all the things that communicate your feelings of love and affection to your future spouse. Then find someone who will do the same for you.

Relational Situation #6: *My girlfriend doesn't appreciate the loving things I do for her. Why is that and why won't she do similar loving things for me?*

The outward expression of romantic feelings should be clearly understood and warmly welcomed by the one *receiving* it. Giving your loved one flowers or chocolate may not be as meaningful to her as giving jewelry. A kindhearted hug may not be as appealing as a passionate kiss. A large surprise birthday party may not be as significant or valued as a quiet, romantic dinner for two. None of these outward expressions is wrong or inappropriate. However, they may not be meaningful to the one receiving them.

> Loving actions must be meaningful to the *recipient* to be considered acceptable demonstrations of love.

When giving someone a gift, what is better received, what you want to give or what the receiver wants to get? Consider the preferences of the *receiver,* not the *giver.* Loving actions must be meaningful to the *recipient* to be considered acceptable demonstrations of love.

If one person loves large surprise parties while the other does not, this may be a source of relational strain. If one person prefers to stay home Saturday nights to watch movies and snuggle while the other person finds this boring, the relationship will have issues. If two people do not share common ground in the area of meaningful actions or activities, compatibility may not exist.

Personalities, likes and dislikes, and life experiences all affect our preferences. When you are dating, discover each other's meaningful preferences and expectations. Then express yourself in a way that holds significance for each other. Or find someone else who has a compatible level of meaningful preference with you regarding the ways you express your love and affection.

Relational Situation #7: *My boyfriend and I used to be romantic and affectionate, but now we aren't. Does that normally happen to every couple over time?*

Barring some medical, psychological, or catastrophic event, people do not mysteriously change. Yes, age, maturity, and life experiences do have an effect on people. However, as a couple walks the path of life together, they should grow closer together, not further apart.

> As a couple walks the path of life together, they should grow closer together, not further apart.

There are many reasons why a relationship (or even a marriage) may not be as romantic or fulfilling as it once was. A couple may find they are not compatible in all four aspects. Perhaps they have not taken the appropriate steps to prioritize and protect their initial connection. Or it could be they allowed themselves to drift apart instead of growing closer. Maybe their careers, hectic schedules, and family responsibilities stole their time together. Perhaps they stopped acting out programmed or learned behaviors and are now just being real.

All these possibilities highlight the importance of complete honesty and discovery while dating. They emphasize the need for compatibility and interdependence in spirit, mind, soul, and body. You can preserve the romance of your relationship by prioritizing it and giving it an appropriate amount of time, attention, encouragement, and protection.

Relational Situation #8: *I express my love in a manner that is meaningful to me. Shouldn't that be good enough for my girlfriend? Shouldn't she love me enough to understand and accept my "love language"?*

According to Dr. Gary Chapman, a pastor and counselor with over thirty years of marriage counseling experience, every person has a primary "love language" by which he or she expresses and interprets love.[47] Here are brief descriptions of the five love languages he identifies:

- *Words of Affirmation.* Love is expressed verbally (hearing "I love you," unsolicited compliments, hearing the reasons someone loves you).
- *Quality Time.* Love is expressed through spending quality time together (full and undivided attention, truly being there, with no distractions).
- *Gifts.* Love is expressed through the thoughtfulness and effort of gifts (gifts or gestures that confirm how highly the recipient is valued).
- *Acts of Service.* Love is expressed through sharing the burden of responsibilities (helping with household chores, lending a hand on projects).
- *Physical Touch.* Love is expressed through physical presence and touch (hugs, pats, holding hands, thoughtful touches).

We all have different styles and methods of expressing our love. As part of your personal development and maturity, identify your love language. It will help you understand yourself and your expectations regarding meaningful loving expressions. It will also help you observe, identify, and try to understand the "language" of your dating partner.

Incompatible languages bring relational strain. If your love language is physical touch, you will be frustrated with a partner who gets little enjoyment from physical affection or expression. If your love language is receiving gifts, you will be dissatisfied with a partner who is unwilling to spend money on seemingly insignificant things.

During the discovery progression of the courtship, identify any "love language" commonalities. Determine whether your communication styles and methods are compatible. Recognize any significant differences before getting too emotionally involved. Ask yourself, *Do I want to experience loving expressions from someone who has to "learn" my language? Or would I rather be with someone who shares the same language and genuinely experiences and enjoys the same expressions I do?* It may not be necessary for two people to have exactly the same love language to be happy together, but you may find someone else's "language" isn't compatible with your "native tongue."

> You may find that someone else's "language" isn't compatible with your "native tongue."

Relational Situation #9: *I've heard love is a decision, not a feeling. Then how do I explain these strong feelings I have for my boyfriend?*

Make no mistake, love is indeed a decision. You make a definite choice when you give your love to someone. You decide when and with whom you will share your life. However, reducing love to a mere intellectual decision makes it feel and sound like a business arrangement.

The statement "Love is a decision" is often said by people who made less-than-ideal relational choices and are now experiencing unfulfilled, emotionally detached relationships. They are desperately trying to fill their inner loneliness and lack of emotional connection while still enjoying the benefits of the existing relationship. They make statements like this to hide their unhappiness and justify their ongoing relationship.

> Love is definitely a feeling. A strong feeling! But it is not *just* a feeling.

Love is definitely a feeling. A strong feeling! A feeling like no other. But it is not *just* a feeling. Love is also more than a decision. In its highest form, love is a continual commitment that is shown by ongoing affection, connection, and fulfillment. It is two people choosing and committing to love each other fully in spirit, mind, soul, and body. They value their love above all else, protect it from the distractions of everyday life, and encourage it on a daily basis.

Relational Situation #10: *Women get into that gushy, mushy, warm-and-fuzzy emotional stuff better than men do. Men are more logical and detached—with strong physical urges.*

Unfortunately, stereotypes exist in our culture today. The general perception is that women are more comfortable with the *emotional* aspect while men focus on the *physical*.

But these stereotypes are not what God intends. Nowhere in Scripture does it imply that women are the emotional guardians while men are the rough-and-tough cave dwellers who are grouchy, detached, disrespectful of women, and focused solely on sexual activity. As a complete and mature man, Jesus exhibited a variety of emotions ranging from tenderness and love to sorrow and tears. Real men demonstrate their manliness by modeling Christ's emotional maturity.

An appropriate balance in all four aspects applies equally to *both men and women*. If either partner emphasizes one, two, or even three aspects at the expense of having all four, the resulting imbalance will eventually lead to frustration, dissatisfaction, relational strain, and possibly a broken relationship. Emotional maturity allows a person to experience genuine feelings and gives the freedom to express them fully.

> An appropriate balance in all four aspects applies equally to *both men and women.*

Relational Situation #11: *My boyfriend may not say it or show it, but I know he loves me as much as I love him. He doesn't treat me as affectionately or respectfully as I treat him, but I know he can change if I wait long enough.*

Many times, we make excuses for our dating partners. We do this because of our strong feelings for them. We skip the spiritual and intellectual discovery process and leapfrog to a strong emotional attachment to someone. We may overlook mismatches in spirit and mind because of the emotional comfort we desperately desire and think we've found. However, even after landing in the *emotional* aspect, we refuse to acknowledge the differences and lack of true connection.

A one-way emotional attachment (dependency) may lead you to believe your partner feels the same way you do. You've made yourself emotionally vulnerable to that person, and it seems safer to believe everything will eventually work out than to face reality and find a healthy relationship with a different person. So you continue to express your love and affection to this person, holding out hope that he will start demonstrating genuine emotional expressions instead of asking what response you expect from him. You believe the day will come when he will connect with you emotionally. You believe one day he will realize what a great thing your relationship is and what a find you are.

This deception protects your feelings and preserves your comfortable *perception* of the relationship. You continue the relationship with the anticipation that the other person will eventually change. But your partner doesn't change. So, in disappointment, you settle for a less-than-fulfilling *reality* with that person, continually hoping he will someday meet your emotional expectations.

> *We are more likely to look for and find a positive view of the things we are stuck with than of the things we're not. It is only when we cannot change the experience that we look for ways to change our view of the experience.*[48]

The reality is that you cannot change or "fix" another person.

> You cannot change or "fix" another person. You can only change your own behaviors and actions.

You can only change your own behaviors and actions. You cannot *will* others to change the way they truly feel inside. Nor can you *will* them into developing the ability to express themselves. People are who they are. They are the unique individuals God created them to be and who they have allowed themselves to become. To expect a dramatic behavioral change is unrealistic. It is also not a wise relationship strategy. You're better off finding someone with whom you share compatibility in all four aspects.

Relational Situation #12: *I'm not an emotionally expressive person. My girlfriend should understand that and accept me the way I am.*

Some people do not consider themselves to be emotionally expressive. Although they may not feel as comfortable with the emotional aspect as others may, very few people live without expressing *some* level of emotion.

Mature emotions are not to be considered an embarrassing, untrustworthy set of feelings against which you must constantly be on guard. They are meant to be fully developed, experienced, expressed, and enjoyed—if they are interdependent with the other three aspects. Emotions are your connection with the experiences of life that surround you on a daily basis.

In a romantic relationship, it is better to deeply feel, express, and enjoy emotions than to simply experience them from a shallow or surface level.

Ocean treasure hunters must do more than just casual snorkeling. They must leave the relative safety of the water's surface and dive into the depths to find the treasure they seek. Very little treasure is found at the water's surface. In the same way, the hidden treasure of emotional connection lies in deeply experiencing, expressing, and enjoying mutual feelings of affection and love.

> Very little treasure is found at the water's surface.

CHAPTER 14

Dating Forward, Not in Reverse

Today's social culture aggressively promotes the *physical* aspect ahead of the other three. The allure and pressure of casual sex, "hooking up," or even having a "friend with benefits" can be overwhelming. However, the world's sexual obsession should not influence, or be the model for, your relationship.

Just because society condones having sex after the first date does not mean that is God's intended relational progression. Actually, God's way stands in direct opposition to the world's reverse order.

God calls His followers to live their lives radically different from the world's norms and standards (II Corinthians 6:17). Instead of blindly following society's twisted mindset, stand out from the world and live your life to a higher moral standard. Resist society's temptation

> Stand out from the world and live your life to a higher moral standard.

and align your search for a compatible spouse with the proper sequence outlined in God's Word. This is the only way to receive God's blessings.

A wise relationship strategy includes the following steps and progression:

1. Develop yourself to full maturity in all four aspects
2. Establish a solid relational foundation
3. When dating, look for (and find) commonalities and compatibility in all four aspects
4. Progress properly through the dating stages—with full physical expression saved for marriage

Levels of Relationships

Fulfillment in an interdependent relationship involves sharing common interests in all four aspects. The compatibility and intensity of those commonalities reveal the potential of the relationship.

For example, classmates or co-workers most likely share *intellectual* interests. They usually have a similar educational level because of the knowledge required for their roles. This makes them good colleagues, perhaps with mutual respect and admiration for one another, but not necessarily anything deeper.

If two people share *intellectual* and *spiritual* commonalities, they may become good friends. They have similar beliefs, values, and convictions. But if there is no deep emotional connection, they will likely have only a surface-level relationship.

When two people share common interests or bonding experiences in the *emotional* aspect in addition to the previous two aspects, they may go to lunch together, hang out after work or on weekends, vacation together, or support each other during difficult life events. They develop emotional affection for each other. They have the potential to become close, lifelong, or best friends.

When these three aspects are combined in a relationship between a man and a woman, their physical attraction may lead to romantic physical contact. They may begin holding hands, playing footsies under a table, fondly touching each other's face, kissing. Their *physical* interaction represents what they think and how they feel in the other three aspects.

With compatibility in spirit, mind, soul, and body, the resulting interdependence is amazing. It gives this couple mutual admiration, affection, intimacy, commitment, and fulfillment. Should they choose to get married, everything culminates in their complete union as best friends, lovers, fulfillers. True helpmeets. Compatible companions.

Building a Solid Relational Foundation

Dating and courtship is more than just a fun and exciting time. It is a critical phase of life when you get to know the people you date and begin your journey of finding someone with whom you share mutual and compatible interests. Dating provides you the opportunity to find a solid foundation for a potential romantic relationship.

Jesus confirms the importance of a firm foundation in His illustration of two men building a house (Luke 6:47-49). He said, "I will show you what he is like who comes to me and hears my words and puts them into practice. He is like a man building a house that dug down deep and laid the foundation on rock." The house that survived the storm was the one with a firm foundation.

There are two requirements for building a relationship that can survive the storms of life.

The first requirement is found in the words *comes, hears,* and *practice.* To solve the mystery of relationships, you must *come* to Christ, *hear* His Word, and put His principles into *practice* in your life. Then follow His guidelines and boundaries regarding relationships.

We find the second requirement in the phrase *dug down deep.* The foundation of a building is more secure when it is firmly attached

> A strong relational foundation takes time and effort. It requires some "deep digging."

to something solid below ground. Digging below the surface takes time and effort. Similarly, a strong relational foundation takes time and effort. It requires some "deep digging."

This deep digging does not mean prying into someone's life for juicy details. It means you use dating as an opportunity to observe your partner from all four aspects. Take the extra time and effort to find out who he or she truly is. Before "falling in love," determine whether you actually "like" this person.

Taking the time to fully discover each other *before* making any significant emotional attachments is a valuable investment. Take the time to be "real" with each other. Avoid spending all your dating time going from one social event to another. Those activities may be enjoyable and exciting. But life usually doesn't mirror such intense social scheduling.

You and your date should talk with each other openly and honestly to identify similarities and differences. It is best to discover any incompatibilities while dating rather than after prematurely and unwisely rushing into marriage. Take your time. There's no hurry. After all, *there are much worse things than not being in a relationship*. You could end up in an unfulfilling, abusive, or dysfunctional marriage and desperately want out.

Godly, Smart, and Safe Stages of Dating

> Attraction and chemistry are terrific. They can also be superficial, short-lived, and disappointing.

Dating usually starts with physical attraction. You notice someone and your heart skips a beat. Yes, attraction and chemistry are terrific. However, they can also be superficial, short-lived, and disappointing. While you may initially find someone highly attractive, upon getting to know him better, you may find he is the most self-centered, obnoxious, or clueless person you've ever met. Physical attraction may draw your attention and spark your interest, but don't let it dominate your thoughts to the point it negatively influences your decisions.

After the initial attraction, relationships should identify commonalities and differences within each of the four aspects. Adhering to the proper dating progression honors God while leading you toward a compatible, fulfilling, interdependent marriage. Following His plan protects each person from unwise and embarassing decisions, uncontrolled actions, regrettable choices, and negative relational consequences.

Considering what we've learned about the four aspects, follow this sequential order in your dating stages and activities.

Dating Stage #1: At this stage, give top priority to talking and observing, discourage any emotional attachment, and avoid physical involvement.

Start your dating effort with the *spiritual* aspect. Although this may sound boring and "holier than thou," it is a critical starting point. We reveal our beliefs, values, and moral standards by what we say and how we respond to situations.

If you are a follower of Christ but the person you're interested in is not, that is the first sign of an "unequal yoke." If this is the case, future dates shouldn't be considered. If you date an unbeliever with the hopes that she will become a Christian, the motives behind her conversion will be questionable. While it is a Christian's duty to witness to unbelievers, it would be best to enlist the help of another Christian who could witness to this person without being affected by "love's distraction." Becoming a follower of Christ is a serious step of faith; it should *not* be dependent on (or distracted by) any dating potential.

If a young woman claims to be a follower of Christ, her dating behavior should align with the high moral standards expected of a believer. She should respect herself enough to hold to that standard and not yield to any physical temptations that a "handsome hunk" or smooth-talker may bring. In the same way, if a young man claims to have biblical values and morals, yet cannot keep his hands to himself, this signals a conflict between his "talk" and his "walk."

Discover the moral integrity of your potential dating partner by looking for evidence of the fruit of the Spirit (Galatians 5:22). Is he or she loving, joyful, peaceful, patient, kind, good, faithful, gentle, and self-controlled? While you're looking, don't forget to look at yourself to see how well you exhibit these characteristics.

Even when both people are Christians, they must then find out if they have common ground on several spiritual topics. Some topics that may affect a relationship include doctrinal beliefs (eternal security, predestination, speaking in tongues), styles of worship (traditional, contemporary, or blended), denominational preferences (Baptist, Methodist, Nondenominational), and church attendance/involvement.

Dating Stage #2: If you find that you and your dating partner share spiritual commonalities, the next stage involves the *intellectual* aspect. As you get to know each other better, find out if you have any intellectual similarities, shared likes and dislikes, mutual life priorities.

Talk about job interests, life purposes, long-term goals, and hobbies. A woman who enjoys knitting every weekend may have little in common with a man devoted to extreme mountain biking. A man who is drawn to art museums or the opera may be incompatible with a woman who finds her thrills attending monster truck events.

A woman with a "doom and gloom" view on life may be exhausting to a man who is energetic, happy, and optimistic. A woman who is undecided about her career, has no plans to attend college, and is okay with a "just take life as it comes to you" approach may view a man who is keenly focused on his college degree or career path as obsessive. A man's indecision or lack of initiative may initially attract a woman's controlling desire; however, it may then be annoying to her long-term.

This dating stage also requires mutual sharing and observing, without emotional attachment or physical involvement. Don't just focus on things you have in common; give differences the same discovery effort. If there is no spiritual or intellectual compatibility, the relationship should proceed no further than an acquaintance or friendship, even if you are physically attracted to each other.

> Don't just focus on things you have in common; give differences the same discovery effort.

Dating Stage #3: If you match spiritually and intellectually, the next relational stage involves the *emotional* aspect. Continue the high level of mutual sharing and observing. Emotional attachment may be increasing, but it is dependent on any mutual connection that exists. Physical involvement should be minimal and sexual activity should not be happening.

In this stage, you and your dating partner reveal more of yourselves as you look for potential emotional compatibility. In addition to what you both are sharing verbally, watch for nonverbal clues from the other person's mannerisms—body language, motions, and inflections. Does your partner maintain eye contact? Smile? Uncross arms and legs when facing you? Lean toward you when listening? Walk closely so your arms and hands touch? Give you undivided attention, even in a room full of distractions? Clues like these confirm emotional closeness and reveal the interest of a prospective partner.[49]

With all the verbal and nonverbal communication taking place, remember the goal is to find compatibility. Avoid "falling" for someone before confirming that the feelings are mutual. Take your time and filter your feelings through your spiritual morality and intellectual reason.

Some couples have a long courtship before they connect emotionally. For others, there is an immediate emotional bonding or "magic" as if they've known each other for years. Even if an immediate emotional connection occurs, a longer courtship period allows both people to truly get to know each other.

Sometimes an emotional connection with another person results from a subconscious comfort level due to familiarity. This explains why some people choose partners with character traits (both good and bad) similar to one or both of their parents. Psychotherapist Elayne Savage explains this phenomenon:

> When you grow up familiar with a certain type of person, you're attracted to that same type of person because it feels comfortable, whether you like it or not. That's what people mean when they meet a potential partner and say, "It feels like I've known him my whole life.[50]

When people grow up in an abusive family, they are at risk to end up in an abusive marriage. They become either the abuser or the victim simply because that is their familiar environment. When children grow up observing their parents' emotionally detached and indifferent interactions, they usually end up in an equally dysfunctional marriage. They become emotionally withdrawn and demonstrate little genuine affection because that is the marital behavior they observed in their parents. This relational cycle is usually not broken unless the children of these dysfunctional situations grow up, recognize the pattern, and consciously choose to resist the familiar.

Listen to the "music" behind the words. To the general essence of the person.

Pay close attention to your dating partner. Listen to the "music" behind the words. To the general essence of the person. Discover what truly makes his heart beat. Learn what she is passionate about. Discuss the fears, the joys, and the sorrows he has experienced or what makes her feel vulnerable. All these experiences are part of who a person is. Listen with your mind as well as your heart.

Along with listening to what is said, take note of what is *not* said. Pay attention to any hesitancy, topic avoidance, or uncomfortable issues. No topic should be forced; however, any reluctance may be a sign that trust and safety have not been fully established. Any hesitation may indicate a relational mismatch or emotional insecurity. It could even signal a lack of true "fruit" inside. If a topic being avoided is important to you and is critical to any ongoing relationship, determine whether it is important enough to terminate the relationship.

If you struggle with putting how you feel into words, maybe you're trying to force something that is simply not there. You must be completely honest! Do not mislead someone just to avoid hurting his feelings. Deception hurts worse than the truth. If you do not feel the emotional connection, say so. If you believe your relationship cannot progress further, your partner will likely experience some heartache. However, it is far better to allow him to retreat as gracefully as possible at this stage, than to mislead each other and proceed with the relationship.

It is at this stage that the decision should be made to either continue dating other people or exclusively date each other. Figure out whether your partner is happy just to be dating or happy to be dating you specifically. If there is no positive emotional connection or the feelings are not mutual, dating other people is a wise choice. Unless you have an emotional connection, interdependence doesn't (and won't) exist.

> Unless you have an emotional connection, interdependence doesn't (and won't) exist.

Dating Stage #4: If you've found spiritual and intellectual compatibility and a deep emotional connection exists, your relationship may then move into the *physical* stage. If you and your dating partner are passionately affectionate about each other, there are appropriate ways to express it. Scripture says, "As he thinks in his heart [the emotions and feelings], so is he" (Proverbs 23:7, brackets added).

If two people feel the same way about each other, they show it. They want to be around each other as much as possible. They mutually express their love for each other without reservation. They enjoy appropriate premarital physical involvement (holding hands, kissing, hugging).

But this physical involvement should be passion under control. You and your partner will need to make the *intellectual* decision to follow your *spiritual* values and convictions and control your *emotional* passions. Mutually agree not to yield to the strong urges you may feel and save your full physical expression and sexual involvement for marriage.

Emptiness, guilt, depression, and emotional devastation are just a few of the reasons more people today are rejecting casual, premarital sex.[51] Even some nonreligious groups recognize the dangers of this sexual trend and have established online resources to "educate, train, and equip, college students with the arguments, resources, and direction they need to uphold the institution of marriage, the unique role of the family, and sexual integrity on their campuses."[52]

> Sex is more than a casual, enjoyable activity between two people. It is the sacred symbol of the intimacy of marriage.

Sex is more than a casual, enjoyable activity between two people. It is the sacred symbol of the intimacy of marriage and is to be enjoyed only within the commitment, security, and honor that marriage provides. God intends sex to be fully and mutually pleasurable—but not before marriage. If you can't control your sexual urges, marriage should be pursued (I Corinthians 7:9).

If the emotions you and your partner feel for each other do not prompt strong physical desires, this may be a warning about physical incompatibility. Discovering differences in this aspect is critical. For example, someone who enjoys passionate kissing will be mismatched with a partner who tolerates an occasional peck on the cheek. A woman who is uncomfortable with public displays of affection will be mismatched with a man who wants to give her a full lip-lock in the middle of a major sporting event and have it captured on the nationally televised jumbo screen. An adventurous woman who anticipates the thrill of making love to her husband while skinny-dipping in the ocean will be mismatched with a man who prefers to keep sex in the bedroom.

Determine your expectations about sexual intimacy and frequency (sex once a day, week, month). Become aware of your intimate likes and dislikes, discover and accept your sexuality, and tune in to your level of physical desires.

Even people who have not experienced sex before marriage usually have some intuition regarding their physical desires. Part of discovering physical compatibility is discussing your expectations with your partner. You may not be able to specifically outline every sexual activity you may like or dislike. But you should be able to identify your expectations. If a man has strong sexual desires, he will be frustrated after marriage to find out his new bride has a prudish view of sex. If a woman expects to experiment with a variety of sexual activities, she will be mismatched with a husband whose view of sex is conservative and traditional.

We develop our preferences in the other three aspects—why would we treat the *physical* any differently? This identifies the importance of self-development and self-awareness *prior* to entering into a serious relationship. In reference to Adam and Eve's

> We develop our preferences in the other three aspects— why would we treat the *physical* any differently?

union, Reverend Billy Graham states, "God wanted them to bring happiness to each other in every way—physically, emotionally, intellectually, and spiritually."[53]

Talking about physical intimacy and sexual expectations should happen *only after* identifying compatibility in the first three aspects and committing to a serious relationship. If either person decides the physical expectations are incompatible and the relationship ends, respect the privacy of your conversations. Maturity in spirit, mind, soul, and body is required *before* you talk about physical expectations. Such maturity also ensures both people will protect the privacy of the discussions.

Physical involvement is not the *only* component of a relationship—but it is an *important* one. During the discovery phase of dating, keep in mind that you do not have to settle for less than your fullest expectations. It's okay to continue looking until you find someone with whom you share complete compatibility—including physically.

Commit to following God's dating progression and avoid the world's pressure to date in reverse. Find compatible levels spiritually, intellectually, and emotionally and save the physical as the celebrated culmination of a married couple who are *Matched 4 Marriage and Meant 4 Life.*

CHAPTER 15

Relational Intimacy

Sharing your feelings makes it easier for others to listen. Listening leads to empathy. Empathy leads to compassion. Compassion leads to intimacy. Intimacy is healing.[54]

The concept of intimacy has been lost in our global community. We expect public officials to share all the details of their moral indiscretions. We eagerly wait for sports figures to hold press conferences to confess their faults. We tune in to talk shows to hear the latest public admissions of wrongdoing. Gossip magazines and news channels are constantly digging for dirt. Even in personal relationships, nothing seems sacred anymore. Women share juicy tidbits of gossip. Men boast about their conquests. All this public disclosure of personal information goes against the very nature of intimacy.

The word *intimacy* implies enjoying a close relationship, establishing and maintaining a deep connection, knowing detailed information, and maintaining the privacy of all words and actions out of respect for the relationship.

Intimacy is a special degree of closeness and trust. It's a level of familiarity possible only in certain relationships. Physical, emotional, and spiritual intimacy are all important parts of health on many levels. They're interrelated with your feelings of wholeness, happiness, and integration into the world. Intimacy is based on trust, unconditional love, and acceptance. To achieve it, you must allow yourself to be vulnerable. Successful intimate relationships among adults are most often encountered in your closest friendships, as well as with your spouse or life partner. Physical intimacy can be very fulfilling. Emotional intimacy is vital to health and well-being. Spiritual intimacy can be seen as an ultimate goal underlying much of existence.[55]

To be truly intimate, both people in a relationship need comparable levels of:

- *Desire* for intimacy. When they both want the same level of intimacy, they protect themselves against the frustration of unmet expectations.
- *Intention* of intimacy. When they both have the capacity and willingness to trust each other, they put forth the effort to become transparent and vulnerable at their inner core.
- *Passion* within intimacy. When they both have the same passionate intensity, it energizes their expression and enjoyment of each other.

Intimacy within the Four Aspects

Spiritual Intimacy

On the surface, it would seem like spiritual intimacy would be the easiest for a couple to achieve. Since they are both Christians and have compatible views on moral standards, values, convictions, and religious beliefs, they can strengthen and encourage each other on their shared spiritual journey. However, to be spiritually intimate, they should also have complementary spiritual gifts, hold similar views on denominational preferences and doctrinal issues, and have comparable life purposes.

Some of these topics may seem trivial; however, any significant spiritual difference will hinder your intimacy. Any differing perspective you discover while dating gives you the opportunity to change your mind on the issue or decide that compromise isn't an option.

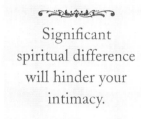

Significant spiritual difference will hinder your intimacy.

For example, if you believe in eternal security while your partner does not, this doctrinal difference will hinder your spiritual intimacy. If your partner believes in speaking in tongues while you do not, that difference will disrupt your spiritual unity. If one person is spiritually mature and has an established Bible study routine while the other person does not, this creates a spiritual imbalance. Any of these can result in spiritual incompatibility. If possible, such differences should be resolved to both people's satisfaction during the initial stage of dating.

Since the *spiritual* aspect is so foundational to a relationship, any unresolved differences show you it is wise to stay friends but not pursue a romantic relationship. Scripture poses the poignant question, "Can two people walk together [truly get along] unless they are agreed [in spiritual agreement]?" (Amos 3:3, brackets added).

However, if both people are in spiritual harmony, they should include God in their activities as they proceed through the dating stages. This keeps a balanced focus within the four aspects. It also prepares them for marriage where they rely on each other's spiritual support.

Spiritual intimacy includes many activities a couple does together. Praying for others and each other. Reading, studying, and discussing Scripture together in addition to their personal devotional time. Attending church and worshiping together. They could also be involved in the same church ministry. As they both mature spiritually and grow closer to God, they may find they are growing closer to each other as well.

Intellectual Intimacy

Intellectual *compatibility* means you and your partner share common ground on a variety of topics. This includes your dreams, ambitions, and goals. However, *intimacy* goes deeper to include your doubts, fears, vulnerabilities, concerns, and views on numerous topics including potentially polarizing subjects. Such sensitive topics include religion, politics, personality differences, and views on relationships in general.

Politically speaking, a liberal and a conservative may have irreconcilable differences. An introverted person may be too "deep" or shy for an extrovert. A ruthless, career-focused investment banker may be too detached and logical for a caring, softhearted nurse. If one person enjoys stimulating conversation while the other person enjoys watching television re-runs for hours on end, the intellectual gap may not be acceptable long-term.

> Without mutually shared interests, what do you have to talk about?

Intellectual differences limit the amount and quality of communication. Without mutually shared interests, what do you have to talk about? Physical attraction and emotional chemistry will only take you so far in a relationship. Mutually engaging and enjoyable conversation stimulates the relationship. It brings vision to the *spiritual*, understanding to the *emotional*, and description to the *physical*.

Intellectual intimacy moves past the talking and hearing of *compatibility* into the realm of truly listening and understanding. Couples who share this intimacy challenge each other to higher intellectual levels while respecting (and listening attentively to) each other's perspectives. Being intellectually matched helps both people understand each other. Having similar interests deepens the intimacy of the relationship because it gives you things you can and want to talk about together.

Emotional Intimacy

Emotional intimacy is what connects two people at a deep level because emotions reside at the core of our being. Genuine emotional expression comes from this core and reflects how you truly feel.

Emotional intimacy is not the same as sexual intimacy. Sexual intimacy can take place with or without emotional intimacy, and emotional intimacy often does not occur within any kind of sexual context. Emotional intimacy is a psychological event that occurs when the trust level and communication between two people is such that it fosters the mutual sharing of each other's innermost selves. It is unbridled mutual self-disclosure. Sadly, a lacking of emotional intimacy in relationships is common, and as a result we pay a heavy price. Its absence can easily be witnessed by way of strained and failed relationships of those all around us, and in a larger context, reflected within the staggering divorce rates. In our most intimate relationships, we seek to feel wholly accepted, respected, worthy, and even admired in the eyes of our mate. We would like our relationship to be a comfortable place for us when we are weary. A place of compassion and support.[56]

We all have a natural tendency to protect our inner selves until we feel we can put ourselves "out there" without fear of rejection, betrayal, or embarrassment. Trust and vulnerability are requirements of emotional intimacy.

> Trust and vulnerability are requirements of emotional intimacy.

It takes time to build up trust in another person; it takes trust to be vulnerable with them.

Trust is required before we will drop our guard, tear down the protective walls we've built up, and let another person in. Reaching this level of vulnerability signals a desire to establish a close connection. We trust our partner not to hurt us, and we expect the same level of trust and vulnerability in return.

The inability to emotionally trust or be vulnerable may be the result of a painful experience or traumatic situation. The death of a loved one. Dysfunctional parental treatment. Domestic violence. Broken relationships with family members. A personal betrayal from a trusted friend or colleague. It may even come from a previous romantic relationship that ended badly. The more emotional pain you have experienced, the less willing you may be to trust and be vulnerable again.

Your life experiences shape who you are and how you interact with others. Thus, it is important to find closure for any past emotional pain. Until you do, and dare to trust again, you are not ready to pursue a serious romantic relationship.

If you have not experienced deep emotional pain, you may not be able to relate to or connect with someone who has. You may be unaware of the fear that resides within that person. You may misread or misunderstand the emotional wall that is raised for self-protection.

For example, a person who has not endured an abusive parental environment usually cannot relate to someone who has experienced this breach of trust. People who have never experienced the death of a loved one typically cannot offer a deep level of comfort to those who have suffered this irreplaceable loss. Individuals who have not suffered deep betrayal from someone they trusted generally cannot understand the lack of trust felt by the one who has endured this violation of loyalty.

People who have been hurt deeply are usually those who have

allowed themselves to be open, trusting, and vulnerable. But, once they learn from and overcome their pain, they are typically more sensitive, understanding, and compassionate than those who have not experienced (or moved on from) emotional pain. Once a person decides to trust again, he may hold a greater capacity for a deeper connection than someone who has safe, surface-level, noncommittal relationships.

A relationship without a compatible level of emotional intimacy may *survive*. But it is doubtful that it will *thrive* or achieve interdependence. How can two people enjoy emotional intimacy if one is loving and expressive while the other is guarded and expresses only superficial feelings? How can emotional intimacy exist if one person pours out the deepest desires of his heart for his partner while she expresses nothing in return?

On the other hand, when both partners are compatible in depth of human experience, passion, and appreciation for the emotional things of life, this connection creates a strong bond. If they share similar levels of *human experience*—the pain, the pleasure, the curiosity, the adventure, the excitement—it enhances their intimacy as opposed to each person pursuing separate interests. If they share comparable levels of *passion*—whether intensely or passively—shared expectations are possible, as opposed to a constant frustration with their differences. If they share an equivalent *appreciation* for the emotional expressions of life—enjoying the inner impact—it promotes genuine satisfaction as opposed to forced or learned participation.

Emotional intimacy and connection may be difficult to explain, but we know when they exist—and sorely miss them if they do not. Examples of emotional intimacy in a dating relationship include:[57]

Emotional intimacy and connection may be difficult to explain, but we know when they exist—and sorely miss them if they do not.

- The ability of both partners to willingly share true inner feelings and thoughts
- Feeling respected, worthy, whole, and accepted—not judged, but mutually enjoying kindness, sensitivity, devotion, understanding, validation, appreciation, admiration, and encouragement
- Enjoying quality time together—simply being together, watching a favorite movie, listening closely to each other, acknowledging each other's feelings with empathy

Physical Intimacy

> Sexual intimacy is the fullest demonstration and most sacred expression between two married people.

Sexual intimacy is the fullest demonstration and most sacred expression between two married people. Presenting yourself sexually to your spouse is the ultimate act of trust, vulnerability, and acceptance. But, physical intimacy in marriage involves much more than sexual activity and you must prepare yourself for the abundant potential it holds.

> *In marriage, God enables us to use our bodies to create a love that is more than the sum of their parts. When a husband and wife put their hearts, minds, spirits, and bodies together with no limits, the result brings a spiritual abundance that—used properly—makes the world a far richer place.*[58]

We demonstrate this level of intimacy by expressing love without attachments or demands. Giving unexpected love notes. Playful touches in passing. Unsolicited compliments. Unexpected gifts. Snuggling on the couch. Spontaneous slow dances by moonlight. Quiet chats beside the fireplace.

Physical intimacy also involves a listening ear, a compassionate heart, a sensitive vulnerability, a respectful attitude, and a shared load of responsibilities.

In his article *Romance and Lifelong Intimacy*, Dr. James Dobson describes ongoing romantic intimacy this way:

> *It is essential to cultivate a sense of romance if intimacy is to flourish in a marriage. Women are inclined to describe romance as the things their mate does to make them feel loved, protected, and respected. Flowers, compliments, nonsexual touching, and love notes are all steps in this direction. So is helping out at home. Men, on the other hand, rely more on their senses in the area of romance. They appreciate a wife who makes herself as attractive to him as possible. A man wants to be respected—and even better, admired—by his wife. Though romance can mean vastly different things to each of us, for most the word describes that wonderful feeling of being noticed, wanted, and pursued—of being at the very center of our lover's attention.*[59]

Creating romantic intimacy for life involves an equal amount of attention and interaction by both spouses. Yes, men and women may differ in their approach to intimacy; however, with mutual desire, effort, and intensity, together they can create the satisfying atmosphere of perpetual romance.

PREPARATION FOR MARRIAGE

The biblical picture of marriage is two hearts beating as one.
Two spirits bonded in values, beliefs, and convictions.
Two minds united in purpose, priority, and emphasis.
Two souls passionately connected at the core of their emotions.
Two bodies fully joined as the symbolic
representation of their complete union.

R U Ready 4 Marriage?

Don't marry the person you think you can live with.
Marry the one you can't live without.[60]

Your quest to solve the mystery of relationships is not over once you find someone with whom you are matched spiritually, intellectually, emotionally, and physically. Compatibility is no guarantee that marriage will miraculously turn into your dreamland fantasies. Along with *interdependence* and *intimacy*, certain *interactive behaviors* are also needed for the daily "give and take" of married life.

> Compatibility is no guarantee that marriage will miraculously turn into your dreamland fantasies.

In order to live these behaviors in marriage, you must understand them, develop and exhibit them in your life, and be committed to them *before you get married*.

From the instruction God gave to Adam, and continuing all the way to the New Testament, we find important counsel for husbands and wives. Scripture addresses specific behaviors to both men and women; however, there is enough overlap in the instruction to presume they apply equally to both spouses. For example, a husband's instruction to love his wife applies equally to the wife loving her husband. Likewise, a wife's instruction to respect her husband applies equally to the husband respecting his wife.

Both spouses fulfill their responsibilities as part of their willing, faithful, and loving interaction with each other. Relationships can't survive with only one-sided effort. Each spouse has a specific role in marriage.

- A husband's role involves loving and leading, providing and protecting. He is to be faithful and considerate, showing compassion and respect.
- A wife's role involves loving and respecting, comforting and complementing. She is to be affectionate and sensitive, showing virtue and passion.
- Together they are each other's partner, confidante, best friend, lover, and soul mate.

Outlined in this section are several marriage behaviors. Some chapters are shorter than others, but that doesn't mean they are less important. This is not an all-inclusive list, but a sampling of the necessary conduct for an interdependent, enjoyable, fulfilling, and lasting marriage.

CHAPTER 16

Make a Lifetime Commitment

A man must not "put away"—arbitrarily leave, forsake, or discard—his wife (I Corinthians 7:11). He must not divorce her simply because he is tired of her, he no longer wants her around, or she no longer pleases him. Although this verse is directed to a husband, the principle applies equally to a wife.

God's intent for a helpmeet is to be a suitable or comparable partner for life. If you properly pursue interdependence and find a truly compatible companion, separation and divorce are unimaginable. If your partner completes you, would you not be incomplete if you leave her?

The word *commitment* means a promise, an obligation, and loyalty. Commitment is not found in the tradition of a ceremony or the symbolism of a ring. Or in a thrilling romantic feeling. Or in the institution of marriage itself.

> Relational commitment lies in your ability and determination to dedicate yourself fully to someone else.

Relational commitment lies in your ability and determination to dedicate yourself fully to someone else.

To become a professional athlete, a man must have the required physical *ability* along with the *determination* to make the team. To become a professional opera singer, a woman must have the required musical *talent* along with the *commitment* to practice her skill.

Before you commit to marriage, search your heart to determine your level of and capacity for commitment. When you handle a complicated task, do you keep trying to resolve it or do you easily give up in frustration? Which mindset do you generally have: "never give up" or "I quit"? Are you mature enough in all four aspects to make a lifetime commitment?

Once you identify this about yourself, discover the commitment level and capacity within a potential spouse. Observe how he handles difficult situations. See if her level of resolve equals your own. Marriage survival requires a mutual and compatible level of commitment.

CHAPTER 17

Be a Faithful Companion

Marriage is a "covenant" (Malachi 2:14). A pact. A mutual promise. A solemn and legally binding contract. It is not something you enter into quickly, lightly, or simply because you have an unhealthy attachment or can't control your physical desires. The vows you exchange are *Meant 4 Life*.

As you prepare for marriage, realize there is to be no deceit or unfaithfulness between a husband and wife. No hidden agendas. No secret habits. No undisclosed bank accounts. Nothing that may be considered a breach of trust.

Please understand one foundational and critical point. Faithfulness in marriage means more than just sexual fidelity. It includes faithfulness in all four aspects:

> Faithfulness in marriage means more than just sexual fidelity. It includes faithfulness in all four aspects.

- *Spiritually.* Stay faithful to your mutual values and morals. Growing spiritually, walking the same journey side by side, and giving each other spiritual encouragement are all part of a healthy marriage.

- *Intellectually.* Stay faithful to your mutual respect and consideration. Challenge and inspire each other. Avoid all unloving or disrespectful treatment that diminishes self-esteem or value (even when "just joking") along with "mind games" to manipulate or coerce each other.
- *Emotionally.* Stay faithful to your mutual connection and completion. Nurture and protect your emotional connection. Eliminate any attachments or activities outside the marriage that provide a competing sense of fulfillment.
- *Physically.* Stay faithful to your sexual purity and intimacy. Avoid all situations and activities that could tempt you to be unfaithful. Respect and maintain the privacy of your relationship.

Keep one serious thought in mind as you go about your relational pursuit. God hates divorce (Malachi 2:16). He intends marriage to last a lifetime. Only infidelity and domestic abuse are two justifiable reasons for ending a marriage. Understandably, irreconcilable incompatibilities discovered *after* marriage can also create an environment in which the relationship is no longer viable or tolerable.

The point here is not to condone divorce. Or to imply you can discard your marriage vows by claiming, "I made a mistake." Rather, it is to stress the serious nature of marriage. That's why it is important not to approach marriage on a trial basis or as an experiment. Take things slow while you're dating. Pursue full discovery in all four aspects. Find a person who is a compatible match *before* entering into marriage. It is much easier, smarter, and less costly to resolve any "irreconcilable differences" while dating than after entering into the covenant of marriage.

CHAPTER 18

Love Unselfishly and Unconditionally

L ove is the unselfish passion of the heart. It involves personal and intimate nourishing and cherishing. A husband is to love his wife as much as he loves himself (Ephesians 5:28, 33).

It is selfishly natural for a man to care for and develop himself in spirit, mind, soul, and body. His instinct is to protect himself, his own interests, and his personal well-being to ensure all-around strength, health, and protection.

Usually, a man spends time, effort, and money on himself, his hobbies, and his interests. He doesn't argue with himself and typically doesn't treat himself disrespectfully. He generally takes care of himself and makes sure that his needs are met. By doing all this, he demonstrates his love for himself. But after marriage, this single-focused self-love should move to a dual-focused love that includes his future spouse. She becomes one with him.

Personal development and maturity involve moving beyond self-centeredness and selfish desires. Before marriage, you generally may do as you please, spend or save your money as you choose, and hang out with your friends whenever you want. You are accountable for your own actions and choices as they affect only you.

> Find and marry someone who you love more than yourself.

But after marriage, a self-centered outlook is no longer acceptable. Your actions and choices will then involve and affect someone else. If you pursue interdependence and find a compatible match in all four aspects of life, your desire should be to please that person. As deeply as you cared about yourself and your own agenda when you were single is how deeply you are to care about your future spouse and her desires. With that thought in mind, find and marry someone who you love more than yourself.

The love a husband has for his wife should be unselfish, voluntary, unconditional, and immeasurable. Within the concept of interdependence, this depth of love applies to both spouses. They should both nourish and cherish each other as much as they do themselves.

CHAPTER 19

Leave and Cleave

Various Scripture verses address a man *leaving* his father and mother and *cleaving* to his wife (Genesis 2:24; Mark 10:7, KJV). The word *leave* in these verses means to leave behind, forsake, or abandon.[61] It refers to a young man separating himself from the first intimate relationship he has, with his parents, and establishing a new and more intimate relationship with his wife. He leaves the comfort zone of his initial family and becomes the leader of a new family by completely and intimately joining with his wife. All previous, present, and future relationships are secondary in importance to bonding with his wife.

Cleaving is a freewill choice that involves full participation and commitment.

The Hebrew word translated "cleave" refers to (1) the pursuing hard after someone else and (2) being glued or stuck to something/someone. So a man is to pursue hard after his wife after the marriage has occurred (the courtship should not end with the wedding vows) and is to be "stuck to her like glue." This cleaving indicates such closeness that there should be no closer relationship than that

*between the two spouses, not with any former friend or
with any parent.[62]*

Traditional American marriage vows include the phrase "forsaking all others." This means more than forsaking other dating partners when you choose a spouse. It involves an ongoing forsaking in deference to the marriage. It means no other person or thing, including parents, children, friends, jobs, ambitions, and hobbies, holds a position of higher importance than this new relationship.

In God's eyes, a married man and woman are not two separate individuals. They no longer have their own lives, agendas, identities, or priorities. Instead, they are "one flesh" (Genesis 2:2; Matthew 19:5; Mark 10:8; Ephesians 5:31). This doesn't simply refer to their sexual union. It means they share an exclusive lifetime together that encompasses their spirits, minds, souls, and bodies. As C. S. Lewis confirms, they are inseparably one:

> *The Christian idea of marriage is based on Christ's words
> that a man and wife are to be regarded as a single organism — for that is what the words 'one flesh' would be in
> modern English. Christians believe that when He said
> this He was not expressing a sentiment but stating a fact
> — just as one is stating a fact when one says that a lock
> and its key are one mechanism, or that a violin and a bow
> are one musical instrument. The inventor of the human
> machine was telling us that its two halves, the male and
> female, were made to be combined together in pairs, not
> simply on the sexual level, but totally combined.[63]*

Marriage is the "glue" that unites a husband and wife. Nothing comes between two things that are glued together. From God's perspective, they are one, and "what God has joined together, let not man separate" (Mark 10:8–9). When we separate two objects, we divide them and create a space between them. In the intimacy of marriage, there should be no room reserved for anything or anyone else.

A spouse brings a level of completion to her partner that no other relationship can. Therefore, neither spouse should ever feel threatened by any other relationship or interest. A wife should never have to compete for attention with her husband's buddies, career, or hobbies. A husband should never have to compete for fulfillment with his wife's parents, shopping pals, or even the children.

> Neither spouse should ever feel threatened by any other relationship or interest.

A husband and wife must be each other's top priority. Things or people who add value to the marriage by strengthening it should be encouraged. Anyone or anything that detracts from it or provides some element of competition within the relationship must be avoided.

A spouse is not merely an addition or extension of your existing life. Nor is a spouse simply a way for you to justify or sanctify sexual activity. Your spouse should complete you in a way that nothing and no one else does.

If you find more enjoyment or fulfillment in other activities and relationships than with your prospective spouse, reconsider your motive for wanting to get married. If you enjoy spending time with your friends more than with your future spouse, you have not prioritized your partner. If you have a closer attachment to your parents or your job than with your prospective spouse, you are not ready for marriage.

The concept of "leaving and cleaving" does not mean you cannot spend time with your golfing buddies or shopping friends. Nor does it mean you can never have any "just me" time. However, all other activities and relationships should have secondary emphasis in consideration of your spouse's desires, feelings, and expectations. Before you are married, be prepared to "forsake all others" and dedicate yourself to the constant pursuit of your spouse's affection, adoration, and affirmation.

CHAPTER 20

Follow His Lead

Submission

Contrary to what some may believe (or erroneously teach), a wife fills a much more interactive role than simply being "submissive" or "co-existent" with her husband. The submissive concept, as taught in many churches, is not God's intended purpose for a wife.

Initially the concept of a wife submitting to her husband may seem insensitive and disrespectful to women. It may even look like it contradicts gender equality. Scriptural terms that reference a wife's submission include "submit to" (Ephesians 5:22; Colossians 3:18) and "in subjection to" (I Peter 3:1, KJV). Titus 2:5 interprets this concept as putting her husband first (CEV) and following his lead (NIRV).

Biblical submission is not a call to servitude or inequality. It identifies relational alignment and implies a wife's voluntary acceptance of God's structure for marriage.

> Biblical submission is not a call to servitude or inequality. It identifies relational alignment.

God introduced this arrangement for marriage after Adam and Eve's sin in the Garden of Eden. When they disobeyed God, he confronted them with the consequences of their sinful choice. He informed Eve that Adam would "rule over" or have authority over her (Genesis 3:16). Paul clarified this relational structure when he said a wife is subject to her husband and the husband is subject to Christ (I Corinthians 11:3).

Christians voluntarily subject themselves to Christ; they follow His lead out of love and gratitude for what He has done for them. In a business setting, there are different levels of authority or responsibility, but each employee is important. On a sports team, each player has a specific role; however, each person contributes to the overall success of the team. Similarily, in a marriage, each spouse has a role to fill as a valued partner in the success of the relationship.

As you prepare for marriage, understand that a wife is accountable to God for lovingly and voluntarily placing herself under her husband's leadership. This emphasizes the importance of finding compatible interdependence *before you agree to marriage*. To paraphrase Proverbs 6:24-25:

> *Ladies, be very selective when choosing the man you will marry. Make sure he truly loves you, respects you, and has your best interests at heart. Do not make your choice solely on the amount of money in his checkbook or the captivating depth of his big blue eyes!*

> *Men, be very selective when choosing a wife. Seriously consider whether she truly loves you, respects you, and willingly accepts this level of partnership with you. Do not be spellbound only by her physical beauty or the sweet sound of her voice!*

Voluntary submission is the wife's response to her husband's love and caring leadership. He loves her and prioritizes her in his life. She responds by partnering with him, reciprocating his affection, and respecting his leadership. Loving responds to submitting. Submitting responds to loving. Since this mutual interaction is easier to achieve when both people are compatible in all four aspects, settle for nothing less.

CHAPTER 21

Take a Year to Cheer

Deuteronomy 24:5 says a husband should take a year away from his duties to cheer his new bride. The word *cheer* means to brighten, to make glad, or to make joyful.[64] A husband is to do whatever is necessary to please and encourage his new bride. After all, she also left the comfort of her family to join him. She has her own fears and concerns about managing this new household and starting a family.

Imagine a new husband taking an entire year to do nothing but spend time with his bride, focusing on what makes her happy— and not just driving her crazy! No job. No outside interests. No extracurricular responsibilities. Simply making his wife his new priority. Affirming her. Delighting her. Moving furniture where she wants it. Hanging pictures wherever she wants them. Doing whatever is necessary to brighten her day.

Considering today's financial demands, taking an entire year away from work might be difficult, if even possible, to arrange. The current-day application of this verse has less to do with finances and everything to do with the significance of the relationship. Both spouses should place primary importance on creating and

> Place primary importance on creating and sustaining a loving, pleasant, and encouraging home atmosphere.

sustaining a loving, pleasant, and encouraging home atmosphere.

A godly husband "cares about the things of the world—how he may please his wife" (I Corinthians 7:33, NKJV). In this verse, the word *please* means to excite the wife's emotions, to be agreeable, or to please her.[65] It emphasizes finding out what makes her happy and then doing it. Even if that includes helping with housework! Starting a new family includes sharing responsibilities such as laundry, cleaning toilets, dusting, vacuuming, washing windows, taking out the trash, and grocery shopping.

A husband who willingly shares in the household chores increases his wife's level of marital satisfaction. This attitude of cooperation communicates his understanding and willingness to partner with her in doing the tasks that are required to maintain a home. This may also increase her enthusiasm to be physically intimate with him.[66]

In the newlywed transition, it is honorable and reasonable for both spouses to help each other adjust to the new home environment. This unifies and solidifies the *spiritual, intellectual,* and *emotional* aspects. It starts the relationship off right. As you consider marriage, prepare yourself to place this dedicated emphasis on your spouse and to demonstrate your committed responsibility to your new home.

In case you were wondering, this concept of "cheering" continues for your lifetime together, not just the first year.

CHAPTER 22

Find Compatible Completion

How a marriage makes both individual lives much better

G od created Adam first, then He created Eve to be his helpmeet. She was made for him, not the other way around (I Corinthians 11:7-9). Scripture does not give a reason why God created them in this order. Or why He made Adam incomplete without Eve. But He completed Adam by providing Eve—and He created Eve from a part of Adam. They needed and completed each other.

Paul addresses this wonderful example of interdependence:

> *Woman is not independent of man, nor is man indepen-dent of woman. For as woman came from man, so also man is born of woman. But everything comes from God. (I Corinthians 11:11-12)*

He explains that the woman came from the man, and man is born of the woman. It takes both people for completion and fulfillment as God intends.

The world holds a skeptical view of the concept of completion. In the movie *Jerry Maguire*[67] Tom Cruise's character expresses his love for Renée Zellweger's character by saying, "You complete me." Late-night comedians and pundits quote this in their attempts to mock such an idea. Promoting self-centered independence, they aim their sarcasm at the concept of finding fulfillment in a spouse.

However, relational completion is not about independence or even dependence, but *interdependence*. You should not be looking for someone to help you *mature* but someone with whom you have compatible skills, talents, traits, strengths, and weaknesses. By doing so, you *complement* each other.

> Compatible companionship is where spouses find and enjoy true pleasure, satisfaction, and completion.

Complementary interdependence involves combining your efforts to arrive at a higher plane of contentment. Compatible companionship is where spouses find and enjoy true pleasure, satisfaction, and completion.

Notice that God gave Adam only one wife. Eve was enough to fulfill the role as his "helpmeet." The seemingly overwhelming task of completing a man can only be accomplished by his wife. She alone is accountable to love and fulfill him in all four aspects.

Likewise, the seemingly daunting task of providing for the needs of a woman can only be accomplished by her husband. He alone is accountable to love her, provide for her, and fulfill her in all four aspects. Together, they need each other and find their completion in each other.

CHAPTER 23

Offer Compassionate Comfort

Abraham's son Isaac grieved his mother's death for a long time (Genesis 24). The intense emotional loss he felt was overwhelming. No one could comfort him. Yet during this period of anguish, life had to go on. So his father continued planning Isaac's marriage. Conducting his own version of online dating, Abraham sent his servant in search of a wife for his son. The servant even had a "wish list" of characteristics the woman had to possess.

The servant found Rebekah and brought her to Isaac. She must have met all his requirements, because he married her and affectionately loved her (verse 67). In response, she loved him and comforted him. Guess what happened next? He was consoled, calmed, and emotionally healed. Something about her affection for him initiated his healing process. Her compassionate comfort brought healing and closure from the grief of his mother's death.

Finding the right spouse involves more than random choice, luck of the draw, or some giddy sense of physical attraction. It takes a committed pursuit of compatibility and interdependence in all four aspects.

> Finding the right spouse involves more than random choice, luck of the draw, or some giddy sense of physical attraction.

It also requires God's wisdom, guidance, and perfect will. In Isaac's search for Rebekah, we see God's sovereign ability to provide the specifically prepared person for any relationship. He providentially met Isaac's relational need. He can do the same for you.

This story reveals the deep connection that occurs when a husband and wife are truly united and intimately bonded. He loves her and she affectionately consoles him—what a beautiful picture of the two-way interaction of an interdependent relationship.

We find a drastically different scenario in Genesis 37. Jacob's sons prematurely advised him of his son Joseph's death. Though his entire family tried to console him, Jacob refused to be comforted (verse 35). Their motives and intentions sought the same consolation, but for some reason their effort did not succeed.

Well-meaning friends and family can provide an amazing support system during periods of grief or personal struggles. Their consolation is deeply appreciated and can have a positive effect. Nevertheless, they do not have the same emotional impact that a spouse holds. There is something supernatural or "magical" about a wife's genuine, sensitive, and loving comfort for her husband.

The person dearest and closest to a spouse's heart holds the amazing power to capture and comfort it. The degree to which this comfort is mutually shared corresponds to the depth of the couple's interdependence in all four aspects. Spirits unite. Minds understand. Emotions connect. Bodies respond in peaceful consolation.

CHAPTER 24

Avoid Needless Machismo

A husband is to love his wife and not be harsh with her (Colossians 3:19). The word *harsh* means to be cruel, offensive to the mind or feelings, or oppressive.[68] The King James Version translates this word as *bitter*. The overall meaning is that a husband must not be insensitive, inconsiderate, or unkind to his wife.

Love is the unselfish passion of the heart that involves a high level of compassion and the absence of harshness or bitterness. In marriage, love is expressed by unselfishly and passionately meeting each other's needs in spirit, mind, soul, and body. Such unselfish kindness and goodwill should be given willfully and naturally.

> In marriage, love is expressed by unselfishly and passionately meeting each other's needs.

A man's harsh language or disrespectful behavior toward his wife is unacceptable. This includes cruel mind games, mean-spirited conduct, insensitivity, or the silent treatment.

Words, actions, or attitudes that demonstrate bitterness include resentment, cynicism, anger, meanness, being unpleasant, and name-calling.

Most of the words that describe bitterness mirror the world's mindset of a "macho man." Someone who acts rough and tough, is untouchable, emotionally detached, and invulnerable. However, the scriptural view of compassionate and unselfish love paints a much different picture than what the world portrays.

An antonym for bitterness is sweetness. *Sweetness* can be described by such words as lovable, charming, appealing, adorable, thoughtful, considerate, pleasant, gentle, softhearted, agreeable, and harmonious.

There is a big difference between a wimpy pushover and a courageous, affectionate protector. Insecure cowards hide behind mean and disrespectful behavior. But it takes a man, fully developed and mature in spirit, mind, soul, and body, to be his wife's loving champion. So men, as the saying goes, *"Man up!"* Drop the tough-guy act and prepare yourself to courageously live a life of compassion, gentleness, and loving affection. Develop and exhibit respectful, sensitive, and honorable behavior in all your interactions.

This instruction against "harshness" applies to the wife as well. Her response and interaction also play a key role for harmony in the marriage. A pleasant atmosphere should be the common goal for two people who are "one flesh." Intimacy and interdependence in a loving relationship cannot tolerate machismo or bitterness— nor exist for long if it does.

CHAPTER 25

Live Peacefully

Pursue peace not war
Don't hold grudges

P aul counsels us to live peacefully, at rest, or in agreement (Romans 12:18; I Corinthians 7:15). This means living quietly and respectfully of others. It involves seeking common ground. Being civil even when you disagree. To do this requires having a calm, mature core at the center of your being.

Preparation for marriage includes peacefulness. Make every effort to live peacefully with everyone (Hebrews 12:14), including your future spouse. Jesus said, "Blessed [happy or fully satisfied] are the peacemakers" (Matthew 5:9, brackets added). There is a direct connection between your happiness and the level of peace you pursue.

Peaceful people are typically not those who must always be right, have their own way, or pursue their own agendas. Instead, they are those who resolve issues through understanding, compromise, and reconciliation. Peaceful interaction involves being considerate, polite, and respectful.

> Peaceful interaction involves being considerate, polite, and respectful.

For a husband, considerate actions may include noticing things about his wife and mentioning them to her in a nice way. Putting the toilet seat back down after use. Using a glass instead of drinking directly from the milk container. Helping clean up after meals (especially after hosting a Super Bowl party!). Taking off dirty shoes before entering the home. Placing dirty clothes in the laundry basket instead of scattering them from the bathroom floor to the bedroom curtain rod. And not field-dressing animals in the living room!

For a wife, peaceful consideration may include respecting her husband's "man space" where he can scatter his "stuff" however he wants. Waiting until after his favorite sports team has finished their game before giving him her "to do" list. Showing genuine interest in his hobbies or projects. Unexpectedly complimenting him. Expressing gratitude for routine tasks he completes, like servicing the cars, repairing the leaky faucet, or maintaining a well-kept landscape. And not nagging him about every little thing that *may* be out of place.

It is hard to live at peace with someone whose lifestyle and behaviors are inconsiderate. When you're dating, observe the interaction between you and your partner. Is it peaceful or do you constantly argue? Do either of you always have to be right or have your own way? When you disagree, do you discuss the issue and seek to understand each other's perspective? Are your resolutions mutually agreeable or does one person generally give in just to end the argument?

If two people are compatible in all four aspects, a peaceful environment should be reasonably easy to achieve. Does that mean they will be in complete agreement about everything or that there will never be any arguments? Not hardly. Each person has differing opinions and perspectives, and those ideas should be mutually discussed. Remember, compatibility isn't about becoming identical clones who always think alike. If two people are identical, one of them may be unnecessary. However, trouble starts when only one viewpoint is considered or when one person stubbornly holds to his or her personal preference.

As imperfect humans, we make mistakes and disappoint each other. A peaceful and harmonious environment includes the willingness to quickly and genuinely say, "I'm sorry," and, "I forgive you." We are not to hold grudges against one another (Leviticus 19:18). Nor should we allow any unresolved conflict to carry over from one day into the next (Ephesians 4:26). True love does not keep an ongoing record of all the things a person does wrong (I Corinthians 13:5).

Every couple needs a harmonious haven. A safe and peaceful place where they can rest together. A refuge from the challenges, chaos, and cruelty of the outside world. This should be the goal for your future home where both spouses peacefully and lovingly interact.

Prioritize and pursue peaceful harmony in marriage. A good rule of thumb to resolve disagreements is to "seek first to understand, then to be understood."[69] The outcome of your discussion may not be full *agreement*, but there can still be peaceful *unity* in the relationship.

CHAPTER 26

Demonstrate a Sensitive Spirit

A wife should not be a brawling, hateful, argumentative person (Proverbs 25:24; 30:23). Believe it or not, very few men want a loudmouthed, abrasive, obnoxious, complaining, hateful, gossipy, in-your-face woman. Even if she can cook and is physically attractive. The world is a harsh and contentious enough environment without such insensitive behavior in the home.

Today's societal standards and our own personal ambitions seem to encourage aggressive and insensitive behavior. "Survival of the fittest" and "the squeaky wheel gets the grease" bring hostility to everything. The belief is that, to succeed or not be taken for granted, we have to be tough and loud. In that downward spiral, women seem to have lost the ability to be sensitive and men seem to have lost the ability to be compassionate. Both have grown increasingly coldhearted in their actions and louder in their demands. They have forgotten God's command to "be kind and compassionate" to each other (Ephesians 4:32).

Yet Peter calls for wives to be "gentle and quiet" (I Peter 3:3-5). Their inner characteristics should be humility, tenderness,

We should focus our attention on becoming peaceful, sensitive, and tenderhearted people on the inside.

peacefulness (a calm spirit), compassion, and sensitivity. These inner qualities are far more valuable from God's perspective than physical beauty, cosmetics, and fashion. "Man looks at the outward appearance, but the Lord looks at the heart" (I Samuel 16:7). We spend so much time and energy fixing up the outside when we should focus our attention on becoming peaceful, sensitive, and tenderhearted people on the inside.

Does this mean a woman is to become a meek and mild pushover? Absolutely not. It actually takes a mature and confident person to be calm and gentle. When the rest of the world is clamoring for attention, rise above the noise. Show your inner beauty and dignity. And look for a compatible spouse who is calm, caring, and compassionate as well.

Other verses in Proverbs identify similar character traits a woman should avoid. Proverbs 25:24 (KJV) says it is better to live alone in a small corner of the roof than to share the same household with a "brawling" or argumentative woman. Proverbs 19:13 and 27:15 compare the nagging and scolding of a wife to the annoyingly repetitive sound of dripping water. Proverbs 30:21-23 (NKJV) identifies a hateful wife as one of the things that "disquiets" the entire world.

A woman with whom a man can share his vulnerabilities and genuine affection is incredibly valuable. This requires a wife with a sensitive and compassionate spirit. A man will not trust his inner self to a woman who is a critical, indiscreet, insensitive, scolding nag. Along that same line, a man must also avoid being hard-hearted and callous in his interaction with his wife. It is difficult for a wife to be soft and sensitive when her husband is an insensitive, "macho" jerk.

One of the components of a successful marriage involves both spouses shutting out the world's disharmony and discord from their relationship. Their goal should be to create a safe haven where they gently love, nourish, and replenish each other spiritually, intellectually, emotionally, and physically.

CHAPTER 27

Live Joyfully Satisfied

A husband should live joyfully satisfied with his wife (Proverbs 5:18). The word *rejoice* in this verse means to be cheerful, happy, and delighted.[70] Most new husbands are excited and delighted with their brides. The anticipation of culminating the relationship with sexual intimacy increases the man's desire for his wife. With compatibility in all four aspects, this should be more than a surface-level attraction or physical enjoyment. It is a deeply satisfying joy for having found "the one" who completes him. He has discovered the missing piece of his puzzle. His companion for life.

This marital satisfaction is part of the abundant life God intends for us to live. The word *abundant* implies a wholesome and joyful satisfaction in spirit, mind, soul, and body. Nothing in Scripture indicates there should be a lack of, or only partial, joy in marriage.

Perhaps you think the concept of "happily ever after" only happens in fairy tales, romance novels, or the movies. But living the abundant life God intends for us to live is not fantasy. Why is it considered normal or acceptable for marriages to grow stagnant, grumpy, argumentative, and detached as the years pass by? Maybe this happens because, when couples were dating, they failed to pursue compatibility in all four aspects. Then after marriage, they did not protect and nurture the initial joy of the relationship.

If you and your spouse each brought ten million dollars to the marriage, you would probably not take your combined wealth for granted. You would focus on your investment to ensure it was safe, earned the most money possible, and wasn't losing its value. The same is true with successful marriage relationships. Neither spouse takes the other for granted. Rather, they focus their mutual efforts on creating an enjoyable environment, protecting it, and keeping the joy in their marriage.

Proverbs 18:22 says, "He who finds a wife finds what is good and receives favor from the LORD." Instead of following the humdrum pattern of many married couples, align your marital expectations with God's intentions. Finding a compatible spouse is a *good* thing—living joyfully in marriage brings God's favor.

As you prepare for marriage, commit yourself to establishing and enjoying a happy marriage for life. Once you are married, plan daily and weekly fun activities together. For example, continue dating. Take mini-honeymoons to refresh your love for each other. Bring home flowers as an expression of your adoration. Remind each other of enjoyable moments from the past. Compliment each other on a daily basis. Use your imagination, creativity, and determination to live joyfully satisfied together.

> We have the free will to make choices in life. So, choose to be joyful in marriage for your entire lifetime.

Since we have the free will to make choices in life, we can choose to be joyful in marriage for our entire lifetimes. So, make the decision that you will enjoy an environment of perpetual romance in your marriage. Find a compatible partner who is equally committed to maintaining an enjoyable atmosphere, then protect your relationship and keep it sacred above all else. Take the time to invest in yourself and your spouse by doing whatever is necessary to keep the freshness in the relationship for your lifetime together.

CHAPTER 28

Show Pleasing Devotion

To truly please someone, you must get to know that person thoroughly. During courtship, take the time to really know your partner. Figure out what makes her happy and unhappy. Learn his needs, desires, and expectations.

When you're dating, discuss what you expect from marriage. If your partner expects five-course meals at home every day, hopefully you know how to cook. If you expect daily back massages, your partner better have strong hands and enjoy a "high touch" environment. If you desire a deep emotional connection, you need a partner who understands what this means and is capable of giving it. Before you agree to marriage, find out if what pleases you and your partner is what you are each able and willing to do.

Paul outlines the competing priorities between single and married people and confirms that spouses should please each other.

An unmarried man is concerned about the Lord's affairs— how he can please the Lord. But a married man is concerned about the affairs of this world—how he can please his wife—and his interests are divided. An unmarried woman or virgin is concerned about the Lord's affairs:

Her aim is to be devoted to the Lord in both body and spirit. But a married woman is concerned about the affairs of this world—how she can please her husband. (I Corinthians 7:32-34)

The word *please* in these verses means to satisfy, gratify, delight, thrill, or give pleasure to.[71] It implies an exciting of the emotions or an intense seeking to make happy.[72]

> Spouses should dedicate their lives to pleasing each other without any distractions from outside their relationship.

Paul encourages believers to be fully devoted to pleasing God in their Christian service. He counsels them to do so without distraction from the world and worldly activities. In the same way, spouses should dedicate their lives to pleasing each other without any distractions from outside their relationship.

The dedication, devotion, and attention of a husband and wife are compared to believers pleasing God by serving Him. Obligatory service or programmed behavior (whether religious or relational) that is performed simply from a sense of duty or responsibility does not bring the same pleasure and satisfaction as does loving and willing action with the intent to please. God is more interested in genuine, heartfelt responses than He is in the mechanical performance of obligatory actions or rituals (Psalm 51:16-17).

This same level of pleasing devotion applies to marriage. Though both spouses have their own mind, free will, and desires, their devotion and priority are to each other. A husband and wife find satisfaction in each other as they both do whatever is necessary to make each other happy and fulfilled. Their mutual goal is to know each other fully and please each other completely.

CHAPTER 29

Create an Affectionate Atmosphere…

Wise Solomon instructs husbands to live joyfully and affectionately with their wives (Ecclesiastes 9:9). The word *joyfully* in this verse means to enjoy or delight in fully.[73] The underlying meaning is to gaze upon her with delight or affection. This implies that a husband and wife should establish a cheerful and affectionate atmosphere.

A present-day interpretation of Solomon's instruction might sound something like this:

> *Be delighted in your wife's presence. Take pleasure in her at all times. Enjoy just being with her. Always treat her affectionately. Spontaneously put on some romantic music, turn the lights down low, and light the fireplace if you have one. Take her into your arms and slow dance with her. Hold her close and look into her eyes. Allow tenderness, compassion, and love to flow from your heart through your eyes and into her heart. Share your endearing thoughts and feelings of affection, both with and without words.*

This affection shouldn't be shown simply because you have ulterior motives. Romance doesn't always have to lead to sexual activity.

Before marriage, a couple's romance is alive and well. They buy each other cards and flowers. They slow dance together. They affectionately touch each other. They talk for hours about everything and nothing at all. They enjoy each other's company. They do all sorts of creative, romantic things together. And this all should happen as sincere sentiments without any pressure or expectations for sexual favors.

> After marriage, sex does not replace romance.

After marriage, the same affectionate expectations apply. Keep in mind that sex does not replace romance. Continue to give each other words of affection and affirmation. Playfully touch and explore each other. Anticipate tender moments just being together.

As you prepare for marriage, determine not to fall into the marital trap of growing accustomed to each other over time. Resolve not to take each other for granted. Encourage mutual displays of affection. Expect ongoing romantic gestures. Emphasize an affectionate atmosphere. By planning for and committing to this type of environment you help avoid relational boredom and the distraction that outside interests can bring to your marriage.

The world outside the home can be a cold, heartless, and demanding place. How wonderful to have an affectionate environment where both spouses can relax, kick off their shoes, lose themselves in each other's embrace, and know they are loved tenderly, passionately, and whole-heartedly.

CHAPTER 30

...Then Be Affectionate!

The Message version of Titus 2:4 reads, "By looking at them [the elderly married women], the younger women will know how to love their husbands" (brackets added). The instruction here is for older, more experienced wives to teach or mentor younger women how to love their husbands.

You may ask, *But isn't love felt? Why should it have to be taught?* The answer lies in the meaning of the word *love*. As used in this verse, it means to be a friend, to be actively fond of, and to demonstrate affection.[74] Since it is difficult to teach something you don't know firsthand, those wives must have personally experienced this level of love to appropriately mentor the younger women.

The meaning here further clarifies the "submissive" role of a wife. It is not one of obedient or obligatory servitude. Rather, it is to be one of friendship, tenderness, and great affection. The instruction for wives seems clear:

> *When you are married, it's perfectly acceptable to throw caution to the wind when it comes to affectionate and physical interaction with your husband. Rid yourselves of preconceived inhibitions. Affectionately, tenderly, yes,*

even passionately love him. Snuggle up in his embrace, hold his face in your hands, look him in the eye, and revel in the moment. Fully experience and enjoy all the moments that make up your lifetime!

When Titus 2:4 was written, the dynamic of marital relationships was much different than it is today. Long-established and generally accepted gender roles and cultural norms did not recognize the fundamental value and equality of women. Back then, women were not viewed as equal with men and wives were considered subservient to their husbands. As such, it would be difficult to imagine a wife feeling very affectionate toward a man who did not respect her as his equal in their relationship.

Paul's new concept of a woman feeling affection for her husband highlights the importance of his relationship guidance. He told men to love and respect their wives. Then he told women that it is acceptable to demonstrate affection toward their husbands. Combine this counsel with Solomon's advice of "Whatever your hand finds to do, do it with all your might" (Ecclesiastes 9:10), and Paul's instruction may be expanded to include mutual passionate expression and enjoyment.

God's intent for marriage is not about servitude, the proper pecking order, or mere procreation. He wants every husband to love and care for the woman closest to his heart. And for every wife to affectionately respond to her best friend, lover, and compatible soul mate.

What is the most appropriate way for spouses to demonstrate loving affection to each other? Is it by keeping the home spotless and orderly? Maintaining a well-landscaped yard? Preparing three healthy meals a day? Performing routine maintenance on the house and cars? Making sure the laundry is clean? While these are all important and necessary activities, don't confuse them with signs of affection. Doing household chores may express *appreciation*, not *affection*.

To tell the difference between an appreciative task and an affectionate expression, ask yourself this question: Could people outside the marriage accomplish the activity (maid, chef, butler, baby-sitter, Laundromat, car wash, etc.)? If they could, then doing it may not necessarily be considered loving affection between a husband and wife. Routine maintenance and household activities are no substitute for emotional and physical affection.

Although it may be expressed in all four aspects, affection is most visible when we show it emotionally and physically—a close companionship of tenderness, understanding, compassion, and love. As matched partners that are meant for life, affectionate expressions should occur naturally and frequently.

> Affection is most visible when we show it emotionally and physically.

Spouses show their affection by spending quality time with each other. Enjoying just being near each other. Surprising each other in ways that bring smiles and laughter. A spontaneous hug. A husband telling and showing his wife that he missed her during the day. Unexpectedly sending flowers. A wife sending her husband a text or e-mail inviting him to a night of pleasure. A husband affectionately touching his wife's face. Enjoying a hot bath together. Gazing into each other's eyes over a candlelight dinner. Tenderly touching and caressing for no reason at all.

Part of the dating discovery process involves identifying your loving affection expectations. Once you've done this, then compare them with those of your dating partner to determine whether they are compatible. Such expectations should include determining your primary method of expressing love,[75] distinguishing a routine household activity from an act of loving affection, and confirming if both have the same desire to create such an affectionate home atmosphere.

A lifetime commitment is a long time for human interaction.

Spending that time creating and enjoying a loving, affectionate atmosphere is as close to heaven as you can get without actually being there. Shower your spouse with tender affection, in creative ways, on a daily basis—and expect the same in return. You'll be surprised how the time flies!

CHAPTER 31

Respect Each Other

A husband should treat his wife with knowledge and honor as to a weaker partner and a co-heir of God's grace (I Peter 3:7). The phrase *weaker partner* does not mean *less valuable partner*. It refers to the unique relational structure God created for marriage (Ephesians 5:23).

By aligning the husband above the wife, God outlined a man's responsibility and accountability within the family. But God never intended this alignment to imply disrespect or dishonor for the wife. With the use of the words *knowledge* and *honor*, Peter refers to wise or sober interaction. This means treating the wife with dignity and respect, not simply as entertainment. A husband should support and protect his wife. Defend her honor. Place his trust and confidence in her. Live with her in harmony and respect.

A man must never use his physical strength or relational role as justification for superiority or abusive behavior. Nor should his male ego be his excuse to avoid showing respect and affection.

> A man must never use his physical strength or relational role as justification for superiority or abusive behavior.

It is hard to understand how some men seem to lose their ability to be respectful and romantic after marriage. While pursuing a woman, a man pays special attention to her, listens attentively to her every word, buys her gifts as tokens of his love, and pours out his heart to her. But once he has achieved his heart's desire, he no longer finds it necessary to be attentive, affectionate, polite, or loving. How completely wrong is that?

A man may be full of bravado and as big, bad, and bold as he wants to be with his buddies, in the gym, on hunting trips, or in all his other interactions. But that is not appropriate behavior with his wife. In a spirit of gentleness, the stronger partner is to restore, protect, honor, and respect the weaker partner (Galatians 6:1).

Even though few men will admit it, deep inside, each man knows his fears, failures, and inadequacies. He may overcompensate outwardly to avoid public detection of his shortcomings. However, his wife should know him thoroughly, yet love him anyway. He should be completely open and vulnerable to her. He should feel no need to present himself to her as something he is not.

A wife should reciprocate the respect and affection her husband shows her. She should not belittle or criticize him or hold him to such a high standard of expectation that he cannot be the person he is. When he fails, she should be his greatest encourager. When he succeeds, she should be his loudest cheerleader.

In the latter part of I Peter 3:7, Peter reminds us that all believers, both men and women, are co-heirs of God's grace. Both are bound for the same heaven. He then warns us that a husband and wife's behavior has a direct impact on their prayers. For this reason, spouses should live together honorably. They should humbly acknowledge the relational structure and responsibilities God has ordained, and confirm their love for each other by their mutual respect and honor.

CHAPTER 32

Give Honor and Admiration

The multiple scriptural references for a wife to honor and respect her husband are directly linked to the many references for a husband to love his wife. This confirms the interdependence between love/affection and honor/respect. A wife is to honor no other man as much as she honors her husband. A husband is to love no other woman as much as he loves his wife.

In the first chapter of the book of Esther, King Ahasuerus ordered his wife, Queen Vashti, to come before him at his banquet. Her refusal was an outright rejection of his kingly command. It was also a dishonor to his request as her husband. Granted, his actions were ill mannered, ill advised, and poorly timed. After seven days of hard partying with his influential friends and nobles, he was more interested in parading her as his "arm candy" than presenting her as his respected bride.

Her choice resulted in the loss of her royal position. After all, the king could not tolerate such outright disobedience. Nor did he want to deal with the negative public opinion should he ignore her dishonor. Furthermore, his nobles pushed the issue by saying:

"C'mon, man! Your wife is setting a bad example for our

wives. She has to go! All the women in the land will hear about her, and they'll be encouraged to mock us by saying, 'The queen didn't obey the king—why should I obey you? You're not the boss of me!'" (Esther 1:16-20, author's paraphrase)

So the king made a new law: "All women will respect their husbands" (Esther 1:20). The meaning of the word *respect* in this verse is to value as precious, give dignity, or to hold in honor.[76]

The setting of this story may be unimaginable from the perspective of today's standards of gender equality and civil treatment. Yet it highlights a scriptural principle regarding the honor, reverence, and admiration a wife should show to her husband. In this story, Queen Vashti was responding to a command from a self-centered king with selfish motives. In our present-day application, we are following a kingly directive for what God expects in marriage.

> A wife's honor proves her love for her husband. A husband's love proves his honor for his wife.

If one spouse does not fulfill his God-given role, the other spouse will have difficulty fulfilling her role. If husbands do not love, it is difficult for wives to honor. If wives do not honor, it is difficult for husbands to love. A wife's honor proves her love for her husband. A husband's love proves his honor for his wife.

Prior to asking her dad, male friends, or neighbors any questions on finances, sports, gardening, automobiles, or any other subject, a wife should first talk about it with her husband. Before discussing a problem at work or a major decision with his mom, colleagues, or female friends, a husband should first talk with his wife. If your spouse does not have the answer to your question or issue, or if it is outside his or her area of expertise, *then* seek the answers from other people. But give your spouse the first shot at it!

Prior to marriage, develop a mindset of honoring your partner. If you have a disagreement, handle it in private, not in front of other people. Affirm your partner instead of belittling or criticizing her. Compliment your partner in front of his family and friends. This will strengthen your connection and will communicate your honor and love for each other. It will also set the stage for such respectful treatment after marriage.

The word *respect* in Ephesians 5:33 is translated as *reverence* in the King James Version. Reverence consists of admiration, awe, love, and devotion. When these behaviors exist, they produce a deep desire to please. When two people truly admire each other, they genuinely want to please each other while trying wholeheartedly not to disappoint or hurt each other.

> When two people truly admire each other, they genuinely want to please each other.

Some ways in which spouses demonstrate their admiration and devotion to each other involve sharing their dreams, ambitions, and aspirations. Seeking and valuing each other's advice. Holding back nothing from each other. Maintaining the privacy of the relationship by not divulging intimate details to others or not discussing each other's faults with friends and family.

A wife should cherish her husband as her earthly protector, defender, provider, lover, and dearest friend. He should be her hero. A husband should cherish his wife as his confidante, equal partner, source of strength, lover, and closest friend. She should be the center of his universe.

When you are dating, look for someone you can respect and who respects you. Instead of a forced or learned reverence, hold out for someone who truly captures your devotion and respect. Settle for nothing less than mutual and genuine honor and admiration.

CHAPTER 33

Rely on Each Other

I t is well known that women are gifted with an acute sense of insight. It is also understood that men can sometimes be impulsive and a bit narrow-minded. Women put their gift of discernment to good use when rescuing men from their ridiculous devices, reckless schemes, and impulsive plans. Periodically, wives must "influence" their husbands with the wise use of their feminine intuition. A wife's intuition can be an incredible resource for keeping her husband from his own stupidity, stubbornness, and prideful risks.

> *"Honey, since you've never used a chainsaw before, let's call a professional to cut down that large tree next to the house."*

> *"Babe, before you buy that motorcycle, let's increase your life insurance coverage."*

> *"Dear, I don't believe skydiving was what your doctor had in mind when he suggested that you become more physically active."*

However, a wife should not rely solely on her intuition. Part of the reason for God's relational alignment between husband and wife came as a result of Eve being deceived and misled in the absence of Adam (I Timothy 2:14).

It was no mistake the serpent approached Eve instead of Adam. The Bible says the serpent was the most cunning, crafty, and deceitful of all creatures (Genesis 3:1). He used his deceptive skills to charm and mislead Eve. To set her up for failure, this sneaky snake started his attack by questioning God's Word. He convinced her to question what God told Adam about the tree—even before Eve was created (Genesis 2:17).

With the benefit of hindsight, a few questions come to mind about the conversation Eve had with the serpent:

- Did she not question the plausibility of a talking snake? Or did she merely accept it at face value as something unique and novel? We can almost hear her say, *Well, look at you! Aren't you the most adorable little creature! And you talk too!*
- Since she was created from Adam's side, why did she leave it? Why didn't she consider finding him to discuss the situation, ask his opinion, or even invite him to enter the snake's chat room?
- What was she doing near the forbidden tree in the first place? Did her curiosity overcome her fear of God's promise of punishment? Why did she linger near the source of temptation?

Instead of outrightly rejecting the tempting conversation, she plunged headlong into it. She tried to explain God's command regarding the forbidden fruit. Eve was not only being deceived, she was freely discussing (and misquoting) something she didn't fully understand, with a complete stranger—a talking snake, no less! When all was said and done, she accepted the word of the serpent over God's Word.

Eve's passive acceptance and naive trust resulted in her downfall. It also led to Adam's sinful choice. Eve was deceived, but Adam willfully disobeyed (I Timothy 2:14). As a result, universal sin became a reality (Romans 5:12-19). Eve's vulnerability to deceit affected the entire world.

Most men have an inherent skepticism and suspicion that is a complementary balance to a woman's trust, acceptance, and enthusiasm. A woman may immediately want to buy a product that's "new and improved," but a man will usually ask for proof or a demonstration before purchasing. Sometimes the roles are reversed and the man's gullibility requires a rescuing lifeline from his wife.

God created men and women with complementary traits so each could be a compatible companion to the other. By relying on each other, spouses keep each other out of trouble. The adage *Two heads are better than one*[77] confirms having a mutual discussion will yield a better outcome than if one spouse acts alone.

> God created men and women with complementary traits.

In your preparation for marriage, be open-minded to consider your future partner's perspective. With mutual love, respect, and trust, each partner should consider the other's point of view prior to making decisions. Your interdependence involves mutual discussions, decisions, and outcomes.

CHAPTER 34

Be a Need Provider

With the fall into sin in the Garden of Eden, man was given the task of hard work to feed himself (Genesis 3:17-19). This is not considered his *curse*, but rather the *consequence* of his sinful choice. When Adam chose to disobey God, God cursed the ground—but He didn't curse Adam. The curse was the weeds and thorns the land started producing; dealing with them was the consequence. Adam's disobedience resulted in extra work to meet his needs to survive.

We live in an age where both genders are fully employable. In view of the rising cost of living and constant threat of job loss, working outside the home may be required for both spouses. However, God gives this responsibility primarily to the man. He is to perform his labor to meet the food, housing, and safety needs of his family. A man who does not provide for the needs of his family is worse than an unbelieving infidel (I Timothy 5:8). The implication is that a husband who fails in this responsibility is untrustworthy, faithless, and someone who has no grasp of the Christian faith.

Unfortunately, some people think financial provision is the husband's only responsibility. At times, men hide behind this misunderstanding to avoid their responsibilities of leading and loving a family. Some men think, *As long as I keep bringing in the money, that's all I'm required to do and everyone should be happy—now get off my back, hand me the TV remote, and leave me alone.* Wrong.

> A man should have a strategy or game plan to provide for his future family's needs in all four aspects.

The word *provide* in I Timothy 5:8 means an advance consideration, or looking out for beforehand.[78] In other words, advance planning. Prior to considering marriage, a man should have a strategy or game plan to provide for his future family's needs in all four aspects. Along with having a job that meets their financial needs, he should also prepare himself to:

- Acknowledge and champion his future family's *spiritual* needs. He should model uncompromised integrity and high morals. Live a godly life that demonstrates his personal relationship with God. Establish the moral standards for the family. Have personal and family Bible reading and prayer. Encourage the development and use of spiritual gifts and talents. Intercede on his family's behalf in spiritual warfare.
- Respect and encourage his future family's *intellectual* needs. He should engage in two-way communication. Share thoughts and dreams. Solicit and consider the opinions of others. Stimulate ongoing intellectual development and aspirations. Help the children with school homework, projects, and assignments.
- Recognize and support his future family's *emotional* needs. He should affirm his love for his wife and children with verbal expressions (saying, "I love you," and, "I'm proud of you) and physical actions (hugging and spending time with each family member). Promote a gentle, respectful, and affectionate atmosphere in the home. Listen to both what is said and

what is unsaid. Be emotionally available to his wife and children. Encourage wholesome living and ongoing emotional development.

- Anticipate and provide for the future family's *physical* needs. He should ensure the safety, shelter, and security of the home. Provide the daily necessities of food, clothing, and personal care. Encourage ongoing physical health and development. Meet his wife and children's physical needs. Enjoy shared fulfillment of sexual intimacy with his wife.

A woman must also prepare herself to share the responsibility of meeting her needs as well as those of her family. She doesn't have to be wholly dependent on her husband. The biblical instruction is that the *primary*, not *sole*, responsibility of providing for the needs of the wife and family belongs to the husband. This does not reduce the wife's contribution or remove her personal accountability for the household's wellbeing.

Christ's relationship with His church parallels a husband's relationship with his wife. As Christ supplies every need of the believer (Philippians 4:19), so the husband is accountable to meet the needs of his wife and children. Not grudgingly, but lovingly. Not as a sacrifice, but as his God-given responsibility. Not as a drudgery, but with a sense of fulfillment and accomplishment. Not half-heartedly, but enthusiastically and energetically (Colossians 3:23 NKJV).

CHAPTER 35

Exhibit Virtuous Value

Proverbs 31 describes the traits of a virtuous woman and gives the sensible instruction for a man to choose such a woman as his wife. The author states that if a man can find such a woman, she will make him truly happy. In addition to this marital advice, Peter encourages everyone to develop virtue (I Peter 1:5). As part of your personal growth and maturity, and in preparation for marriage, make sure you include the essential trait of virtue.

In Proverbs 31:10, the meaning of the word *virtuous* is having valor, strength, and substance.[79] Virtue is defined as having moral excellence, right action and thinking, goodness or morality, and chastity.[80] Synonyms of virtuous are good, righteous, worthy, honorable, moral, upright, and honest.[81]

> Virtue is moral excellence, right action and thinking, goodness or morality, and chastity.

In reviewing these verses, Matthew Henry's *Commentary on the Whole Bible*[82] reveals a virtuous woman has the following characteristics:

- *She is chaste, modest, and discreet.* Her behavior exhibits discretion and integrity. Her conversation is sensible, prudent, and careful. She gives no reason or basis for jealousy, doubt, or disrespect.
- *She is diligent and frugal.* She manages her resources in such a manner that there is always enough to meet the needs of her family. She gives no cause for lack, envy, or constantly needing more.
- *She is devoted to her husband.* Her attentiveness to him demonstrates his place of primary importance in her life. Her interaction with him contributes to his completion by knowing him intimately. She anticipates his needs and meets them fully. She gives him no reason or desire to seek fulfillment elsewhere.
- *She is attentive to her family.* Her dedication to them ensures their needs are met and their priorities are maintained. Her sense of practicality ensures their needs are met without falling prey to the prevailing fads, fashion, or societal trends. She gives them no reason for dysfunctional behavior or disloyalty of any kind.
- *She is committed to her children's development.* Her involvement and guidance ensures that each child is loved, disciplined, valued, affirmed, and encouraged to full maturity into the adults God intends them to be. She gives no reason for them to feel embarrassment or fear as they interact with the world.
- *She is mindful of her responsibility to God.* Her spiritual development and insight reveal her personal relationship and growing fellowship with Him. She demonstrates her dedication to pleasing Him in her faithful interaction with her husband, her immediate family, her extended family, and others in her social network. She gives no reason for blame or shame to herself, her family, or to the cause of Christ.

Does this seem too good to be true? Does it sound like the idealistic pursuit of the perfect woman? Clearly, God does not dangle tantalizing things in front of us to tease, torment, or frustrate us.

He provides His Word as our instruction manual to reveal the possibilities of our full potential. We should trust Him, believe that He gives His counsel for our benefit, and pursue the blessings He offers.

Does this virtuous checklist sound like a huge responsibility for one person? Absolutely. But nowhere in Scripture is anyone encouraged to be average, to not give his best effort, to not become all that she can be. Actually, Scripture tells us to do everything with *all* our might (Ecclesiastes 9:10) and with *all* our heart (Colossians 3:23).

Notice the interdependence. The virtuous woman directs her time, attention, affection, and energy toward her husband and family. Her husband responds by loving her, providing for her, respecting her, reflecting pride to be her husband, and reciprocating her expressions of affection toward him. Each spouse finds completion and fulfillment in the expressions, interactions, and deeds of the other.

CHAPTER 36

Be Ravishingly Captured

Solomon paints a beautiful picture portraying the pleasure and satisfaction of a married couple enjoying the *physical* aspect:

> *Let thy fountain be blessed: and rejoice with the wife of thy youth. Let her breasts satisfy thee at all times; and be thou ravished always with her love (Proverbs 5:18-19,* KJV*).*

Although he references a woman's breasts, the overall implication is not limited to a specific part of the female body. Instead, it refers to the complete experience of sexual intimacy that a wife shares with her husband.

Two words in verse 19 deserve our attention:

- *Satisfy.* It implies the quenching of thirst. The satiating of an appetite. An abundant filling of something strongly desired.
- *Ravished.* It means to be captivated or mesmerized. Brought under the spell or intoxicating influence of something.

Both words describe powerful influencers. Consider these comparisons. A refreshing drink of cold water on a hot, dry day. A satisfying meal when hungry. Being under the intoxicating influence of an alcoholic beverage. That is the effect a wife's physical love should have on her husband.

You did notice how the verse says that, right? It says the husband should be ravished, enraptured, intoxicated with *his wife's* love. It is not the husband's love that initiates ravishing satisfaction. It is the love that the wife fully and actively shares with her husband that has this captivating effect on him.

Ravishing satisfaction does not describe an obligatory act. Nor does it portray sexual activity that is highly pleasurable to one spouse while merely being tolerated by the other. Both spouses are to enjoy each other physically, with intoxicating passion and quenching satisfaction. It should be so powerful that they have no interest in seeking physical pleasure outside the marriage. No stolen moment of premarital or extramarital physical pleasure can match the ravishing and pleasurable satisfaction God intends for marriage.

> The power of the *physical* aspect finds its core connection in the *emotional* aspect, its determined commitment in the *intellectual* aspect, and its blessing in the *spiritual* aspect.

A married couple's physical union causes the rest of the world to grow distant and silent. No other priority captures their interest. No other tempting call distracts their attention. Spirit, mind, soul, and body are captivated by the physical love they share. The power of the *physical* aspect finds its core connection in the *emotional* aspect, its determined commitment in the *intellectual* aspect, and its blessing in the *spiritual* aspect.

As you prepare for marriage, set the expectation that both spouses should equally initiate physical and sexual intimacy. In this way, you maintain an atmosphere of perpetual romance where both spouses are ravishingly "intoxicated" with each other.

CHAPTER 37

Enjoy Sexual Expression

One of the provisions for marriage is to avoid sexual immorality. Husbands and wives are to give each other "due benevolence" (I Corinthians 7:3, KJV). Other versions interpret this as "reciprocal affection" (NKJV), a "balanced and fulfilling sexual life" (Msg), and "shared conjugal rights" (AMP). In other words, both spouses are to fully interact with and enjoy *physical* intimacy.

Sadly, some churches present sexual intimacy as a woman "meeting her husband's needs" or "fulfilling her wifely duty" as if to imply a woman has no sexual needs of her own. Sex is viewed as dirty, carnal, and unspiritual. These views stand in direct opposition to what God says about it. If there is no pleasure, enjoyment or emotional connection, sexual interaction becomes nothing more than a physiological release.

Spouses who find pleasure in their spiritual, intellectual, and emotional compatibility should also mutually enjoy and actively participate in physical intimacy. This is the crowning interaction where both spouses fully and freely express what they think and how they feel toward each other.

Please allow a few analogies that bring to life the importance of full involvement and expression in the *physical* aspect. A lamp benefits no one unless it is *turned on*. A microwave will not cook anything unless it is *turned on*. A car goes nowhere unless it is *turned on*. As a matter of fact, without the charge or energy flow from the battery, a car's engine will not even start. The point being—things do not function properly without the required level of energy. The same holds true for sexual intimacy in marriage. When you are married, arouse your sexual passion, release all self-control, and mutually enjoy the intimate pleasure!

> When a husband and wife find fulfillment in each other, sexual intimacy becomes a part of who they *are*, not just something they *do*.

When a husband and wife find fulfillment in each other, sexual intimacy becomes more than marital duty, relational obligation, or a simple physical act. Instead, sexual intimacy becomes:

- A part of who they *are*, not just something they *do*
- The highest expression of who they are together, not simply what they do if one or the other "gets lucky"
- An atmosphere of perpetual romance, not a reward system where good behavior results in sexual favors
- The constant outward expression of their mutual love and passion

Paul clarifies that neither the husband nor the wife have authority over his or her body (I Corinthians 7:4). Upon getting married, they mutually give that power to each other. The instruction Paul gives is to not "defraud" one another (I Corinthians 7:5, KJV). This means not to refuse, deprive, or withhold sexual intimacy from each other. There should be no holding back, embarrassment, fear, improper inhibitions, or misguided perceptions that sexual activity is something to be tolerated.

Men, as you prepare for marriage, develop an honorable mindset regarding your intimate interactions with your future wife. Once you are married, it is shameful to expect sexual intimacy from your wife if you are not emotionally supportive, loving, and respectful of her. If you expect her time and attention at night, plan on spending time with her during the day. If you expect her pleasure in the bedroom, plan on helping her with the housework in the other rooms of the house. If you treat her disrespectfully, then expect her to hesitate or avoid physical intimacy.

Women, as you prepare for marriage, create a similar mindset. As a wife, it is appalling to simply endure or go through the motions of sexual activity with your husband. To do so is not honoring, affirming, or loving. It reveals you are not emotionally connected and fully expressive with him. If your mind has the ability to multitask, discipline yourself to avoid this distraction during physical and sexual intimacy. If you expect to hear his "sweet nothings" at night, plan on letting him hear your words of loving affirmation throughout the day. If you're not emotionally and passionately involved in the moment, then expect him to be frustrated and distant.

Physical fulfillment involves more than simply going through the motions of sexual activity. The Bible tells us, "Whatever you do, work at it with all your heart" (Colossians 3:23). The word *all* in

> Both spouses should fully experience and intimately enjoy physical pleasure.

this verse doesn't just apply to our focus and effort in the *spiritual*, *intellectual*, or *emotional* aspects. It confirms that God intends for the *physical* aspect to get as much emphasis as the others. As a part of the abundant life He expects us to live, both spouses should fully experience and intimately enjoy physical pleasure as their expression of complete love for each other.

CHAPTER 38

Being Versus Doing

Interdependence in a compatibly matched relationship is more about *being* than *doing*. It is about simply *being* with another person instead of necessarily *doing* things together. It is each person feeling comfortable just being himself and both people enjoying who they are together. It is feeling safe and content with the nearness and presence of the person you love.

Sure, doing things and going places together is thrilling, memorable, and enjoyable. However, all that can be experienced with *anyone*. Activities and events do not make a relationship special; people do. The man and woman within the relationship make it (and the corresponding activities) truly amazing. Their individual uniqueness, shared compatibility, and connection, make the relationship extraordinary. This "extraordinariness" makes what they do more meaningful and enjoyable.

> Activities and events do not make a relationship special; people do.

Luke 10:38-42 vividly portrays the difference between *being* and *doing*. In this story, we find Jesus spending time with his friends Lazarus, Mary, and Martha. Mary was content just *being* in the presence of Jesus. Listening to Him. Being near Him. Sharing the moment with Him. Jesus, her dearest friend, was in their home. The man who healed the sick. Made the blind to see. Cast out demons. Turned water into wine. Fed thousands with a boy's lunch. Was relentlessly pursued by massive crowds. *And He was in the house!*

Martha, meanwhile, was "cumbered about much serving" (verse 40, KJV). The New King James Version says she was "distracted" with all the activities involved in hosting and entertaining guests. There was food to prepare. The house to clean. Tables to arrange. Servants to manage. She was an anxious and conscientious hostess who was focused on *doing.*

Was Martha wrong for ensuring everything was in order? Of course not. From an *organizational* perspective, these things were necessary. But from a *relational* perspective, they should have been secondary in importance to spending time with Jesus. Jesus gave Martha some insight regarding her worry and trouble about "many things" compared to Mary's time spent with Him. He said, "One thing is needed, and Mary has chosen that good part, which will not be taken away from her" (Luke 10:42 NKJV).

As you prepare for marriage, consider this. There will always be meals to prepare, the house to clean, and guests to entertain. There will always be laundry to wash, vacation spots to enjoy, and e-mails to send. There will always be sporting events to attend, hobbies to enjoy, and television shows to watch. There will always be newspapers to read, Web sites to surf, the lawn to mow, and cars to wax. But *doing* all these activities, even if they're done together, doesn't replace *being* together—in the moment, connected in the present reality. Future moments may never arrive; activities come and go. Meaningful time together is a precious and fleeting resource.

Mary chose to spend time with Jesus. Martha chose to let that relational opportunity pass her by, never to return. The impact of their opposite choices is the difference between entertaining and enjoying, duty and devotion, seeking approval and giving adoration, *doing* and *being*.

Too often we mistake *doing* things together for *being* together. A couple can *do* many things together without truly *being* together. They may perform all the activities in the world, but their hearts and minds may be worlds apart.

> Too often we mistake *doing* things together for *being* together.

Busyness is no substitute for connection and intimacy. The daily requirements of life demand so much of our attention, it is easy to lose focus on what is truly important. Your compatible mate deserves your undistracted time, active presence, engaged involvement, and established priority.

When you are dating, create a *being* mindset. Truly get to know, appreciate, and connect with your future spouse. Prepare yourself for a marriage that includes *being* present with each other and not simply settling for *doing* many things together.

SOLVING THE MYSTERY

Husbands, love your wives,
just as Christ loved the church
and gave himself up for her
(Ephesians 5:25)

Love the Lord your God
with all your heart,
with all your soul,
with all your mind,
with all your strength.
(Mark 12:30)

CHAPTER 39

The Mystery Solved

We find an important clue for our quest to solve the mystery of relationships in Ephesians 5:25. A husband should love his wife the same way Christ loved the church (His followers; believers) and gave Himself for it. The meaning behind the word *gave* in this verse means to surrender, commit, entrust, or yield.[83]

Christ humbly served others even though He is the head of the church. His primary purpose was to give His life for the world. He did not come to earth to be waited on or to pursue His own desires. He served others, helped them when they could not help themselves, and looked out for their best interests (Matthew 20:28). He sacrificed His life for His followers so they could be free from the controlling effect of sin and live the abundant life He wants them to live (John 10:10).

The primary responsibility of a husband is to meet his wife's needs lovingly, respectfully, affectionately, and faithfully. He is to dedicate his time, energy, attention, focus, purpose, motivation—his all—to her. Keep in mind that Christ continues to love the church even when she acts unlovable, strays from close fellowship with Him, and even treats Him with indifference.

However, to keep this from feeling a bit one-sided, there is a second critical clue that applies to a wife. Using the same example of husbands loving their wives as Christ loved the church, ask yourself, *What did Christ tell the church?*

> Love is the unselfish passion of the heart, involving deep compassion and a choice of the will. It is demonstrated through passionate acts by a committed heart.

In Mark 12:30, Jesus gave a new commandment to His followers: to love the Lord with all their heart, mind, soul, and strength. The word *love* in Mark 12:30 refers to a direction of the will and finding one's joy in the person being loved.[84] This love is the unselfish passion of the heart involving deep compassion and a choice of the will. It is demonstrated through passionate acts performed by a committed heart. It requires a daily choice to love completely, unselfishly, and passionately.

The word *heart* in this verse refers to the core of human sentiment. This correlates to the *emotional* aspect. The words *mind* and *soul* correspond to the *intellectual* and *spiritual* aspects. The word *strength* refers to *physical* power and ability. To fully experience Christ's abundant life, we are to love Him spiritually, intellectually, emotionally, and physically. All four aspects are to be equally present and fully engaged.

In applying this spiritual comparison to marriage, we find that a wife is to be equally, wholly, and lovingly interactive with her husband—spirit, mind, soul, and body. This involves her reciprocal response to the complete love her husband gives her. Just as faith without corresponding action is dead (James 2:17), so love without a reciprocal response is frustrating, unfulfilled, and meaningless—*lifeless*.

With all four aspects in place, interaction in marriage can hardly be described as sacrificing or in need of "being worked on." If two people truly love each other, no sacrifice is too large and no request is too small. Each person is totally committed to fulfilling the other.

> If two people truly love each other, no sacrifice is too large and no request is too small.

If, while dating, the relationship does not hold an unselfish level of two-way interaction and priority, a future together could very well lead to a life of continually sacrificing and "working things out." This should be a cause for pause in the progression of the relationship.

Before you consider marriage and the beauty, fun, and pleasure it brings, seriously consider Christ's modeled behavior. Marriage is about putting your spouse's needs first, not being waited on hand and foot. It is about personal sacrifice for the benefit of your spouse and family, not about having your own personal agenda and lifestyle. It is about giving of yourself—even laying down your life if necessary—for the protection and provision of your spouse and children. When you are prepared and committed to do so without hesitation, you are ready for marriage.

Consider your dating partner from this perspective. As Christ loves the church completely, so husbands should fully love their wives. As the church loves Christ, so wives should love their husbands with all their heart, mind, soul, and body.

The mystery of a man and a woman is solved when both people in a relationship fulfill their corresponding roles. A husband and a wife are to love each other with *all* their hearts, minds, souls, and bodies. Compatibly. Faithfully. Unconditionally. Passionately. Interdependently.

CHAPTER 40

Your Heart's Desire

*"Nothing brings more joy than a good marriage, and
nothing brings more misery than a bad marriage."*[85]

In the final analysis, the "mystery" comes down to a fairly easy personal question. What is the sincerest, deepest desire of your heart? To answer this, consider these questions. What degree of interaction do you want in your marriage? What level of intimacy in marriage do you want and are you prepared to create it? How patient and persistent will you be in finding compatibility in all four aspects? Are you truly interested in finding interdependence? Or do you simply want to continue doing what's been done before and risk having your relationship efforts ending up as a negative statistic?

> What is the sincerest, deepest desire of your heart?

If your heart's desire is marriage, what is your true reason for pursuing such a relationship? There are many misguided motives for wanting to be married. They all miss the mark and can result in heartache, unfilled expectations, miserable lives, and possibly even divorce and a broken home.

Think about the following reasons people have for wanting to get married as well as the candid responses to those reasons:

- Do you want someone with whom to see the world and visit entertaining places? If so, ask a travel agent to book you on a group tour.
- Do you simply want someone to have an outlet for your sexual urges? Shame on you!
- Do you want someone to make you laugh and share exciting times? Hire a clown.
- Do you want to have and raise children? Call an adoption agency.
- Do you want to simply coexist with someone? Stay with your parents, siblings, or extended family.
- Do you want a constant companion who tolerates you no matter what? Get a pet.
- Do you want someone who will listen to you? Volunteer as a teacher at your church or as a reader at a local school.
- Do you want to spend most of your time on household chores? Hire yourself out as a maid.
- Do you want someone with whom to argue your point of view? Join a debate club.
- Do you want some one-sided affirmation? Call a support hotline.
- Do you want someone to share life's expenses? Get a roommate.
- Do you want to enjoy social status? Get involved with your community, support the performing arts, or join the chamber of commerce.

There are many outlets for all these reasons that will fulfill your developmental, experimental, creative, or thrill-seeking pursuits. *But they do not require marriage.*

However, if the true desire of your heart is to enjoy a satisfied, fulfilling, and abundant life with a compatible spouse, with whom you share an intimate journey filled with mutually enjoyable experiences, then look for the person uniquely matched with you in spirit, mind, soul, and body.

We've followed the clues; the mystery of relationships has been solved. A genuinely satisfying and lasting marriage can be found. The fulfillment, thrilling companionship, and pure ecstasy of life-long perpetual romance all await you. Are you up to the challenge? With compatibility and balanced interdependence in all four aspects, proper progression through the dating stages, God's guidance, and your patience, you can find your special someone with whom you are *Matched 4 Marriage and Meant 4 Life*!

Compatibility Checklist

Putting together the pieces of your life's "puzzle" can be challenging and maybe even a bit scary. This section should help you honestly assess yourself and identify the relational characteristics most suitable for your unique personality and situation. As you complete and review this checklist, keep in mind that other people are also looking for their missing "puzzle piece." Ask yourself if the person you're looking for would also be looking for someone like you.

When considering these characteristics, separate those that are definite *needs* from those that may be *optional but preferred*. Consider strengths, weaknesses, and requirements as you assess yourself as well as a potential partner. Clearly outline the traits you find most and least attractive in a companion.

The *strengths* you identify should be your characteristics that bring value to a romantic relationship. List those qualities in which you have a high comfort level—with either how you view yourself or how you interact with others. These traits should complement those of a potential spouse and may be strengths he or she may want or need in a relationship.

The *weaknesses* you identify should be characteristics you currently do not have, may never have, or that should be resolved before you pursue a romantic relationship. List any behaviors or traits in which you have a low degree of comfort—in how you view yourself and how you interact with others. These areas of improvement reveal your opportunities for growth as well as traits that may be offset by a potential spouse's strengths.

> Don't look for someone who is perfect—look for the one who is perfect for you.

The *requirements* in a compatible spouse should identify what you feel is necessary to be fully satisfied and fulfilled in your future married life. Decide which things are nonnegotiable "needs" and which are optional "wants." You may wish to rate the optional qualities by level of preference. Be honest, but be realistic. Don't look for someone who is perfect—look for the one who is perfect for you (and who thinks the same about you!). Be careful not to allow an imbalance or overemphasis in any of the four aspects to convince you to settle for less. Take your time and wait until you find "the right one!"

Spiritual Aspect

List three to five of your spiritual *strengths*. These may include a deep personal faith. Living in agreement with religious beliefs. A strong sense of morals, standards, and convictions. A belief in an absolute authority versus relativism. A keen sense of wrong and right. Enjoying a personal and vibrant relationship with Jesus Christ. (For example, you may write, *I am a born-again Christian with a Southern Baptist background. I do my best to follow the Bible's morals and standards of behavior. I will not compromise my integrity for momentary physical pleasure outside of marriage.*)

_____

_____

_____

List three to five of your spiritual *weaknesses* or areas of improvement. These may include a tendency to let feelings of the moment and "situational ethics" determine your moral standards. Having little or no spiritual depth. Spending little time reading the Bible, study guides, or devotionals. (For example, *I try to read the Bible every day, but sometimes find it boring. I do not attend church every week. I believe "religion" is too personally restrictive. I view "churchy" people as judgmental, guilt-ridden hypocrites who have no fun. But when I push against moral and ethical boundaries, I realize I would have been better off following God's laws.*)

List three to five spiritual *requirements* you are looking for in a potential mate. These may include being of the same faith or denomination. Holding similar moral standards or convictions. Sharing an equal level of interest and intensity in spiritual matters. Having a daily walk that mirrors spiritual talk. (For example, *My ideal mate is a Christian who does not smoke, drink, dance, or gamble. She lives a moral lifestyle in agreement with her faith, but is not a legalistic hypocrite. She knows how to have fun in morally upright ways. She demonstrates love and compassion for others by volunteering to help with the elderly, offering food to the homeless, working in prison ministry, or going on missions trips. She enjoys discussing the Bible with me and discovering new spiritual insights together.*)

_____

_____

_____

Intellectual Aspect

List three to five of your intellectual *strengths*. These may include educational pursuits or professional certifications. Activities that stimulate your mind and thought process. Career experiences. Decision-making skills. Integrity, wisdom, and common sense. Money management. (For example, *I have a degree in engineering and work in a highly technical field. Though I make a good living, I tend to be frugal with my money to make it stretch. I think about decisions for a long time before coming to conclusions, considering all the consequences I can foresee. I plan ahead for just about everything in my life. I consider myself a commonsense, down-to-earth person. I enjoy reading nonfiction biographies, listening to classical music, and having small groups of friends over from time to time. Traveling to historically significant sites is exciting—amusement parks annoy me.*)

_____

_____

_____

_____

_____

List three to five of your intellectual *weaknesses* or areas of improvement. These may include focusing too much on physical attraction. Poor communication skills. A low comfort level with social graces. Indecisiveness. Inability to speak your mind. Lack of self-confidence. (For example, *I am an intellectual snob who is impatient with others who do not readily grasp commonsense concepts. I sometimes look down on people who are not college graduates. I tend to be impatient with people who don't see things the way I do. I cannot always express myself clearly enough to make sure I am understood. I get bored with those I perceive are "beneath me" intellectually. I have a tendency to be intolerant of viewpoints different from mine.*)

List three to five intellectual *requirements* you are looking for in a mate. These may include being an educated or professional individual. Career commonalities. A witty sense of humor. Easygoing personality with a strong sense of self-confidence. A certain lifestyle you wish to live. (For example, *My ideal mate works hard, but doesn't bring his job home. He enjoys sightseeing with me on the weekends. He has a dry, intelligent sense of humor. He is open to discussing new ideas and fresh approaches to life's situations and issues. With our career choices, we will be able to provide the lifestyle we are seeking.*)

Emotional Aspect

List three to five of your emotional *strengths*. These may include intuitiveness. Sensitivity to others' well-being. Emotional depth or maturity. A well-established confidence with yourself. A high comfort level with expressing and demonstrating your feelings. (For example, *I am an emotionally stable person with a generally positive disposition and outlook on life. I like who I am. I am comfortable expressing a variety of feelings without fear of embarrassment or rejection. I am not ultra-sensitive to criticism.*)

_____

_____

_____

_____

_____

List three to five personal *weaknesses* or areas of improvement within the emotional aspect. These may include maintaining an inwardly focused perspective. Being shallow and insincere. Being more of a "taker" than a "giver." Having a selfish or inwardly focused perspective. Feeling uncomfortable about expressing emotions. Having difficulty trusting and being vulnerable with people. (For example, *Too often, I depend on others for affirmation. I am embarrassed to cry in front of people. I usually have difficulty sharing my feelings with others or allowing them to know the real me. I am prone to unexplained mood swings that negatively affect others as well as me.*)

_____

_____

_____

_____

_____

List three to five emotional *requirements* you are looking for in a mate. These may include being able and willing to share innermost feelings without being prompted. Being open, honest, vulnerable, and in tune with your inner self. Demonstrating mature behavior. (For example, *My ideal mate is comfortable expressing his feelings. He does not shut me out when he is having troubles. He anticipates my needs and tries to meet them before I ask. He is not dependent on me or independent from me, but seeks emotional interdependence with me.*)

_____

_____

_____

_____

_____

Physical Aspect

List three to five of your physical *strengths*. These may include knowing what you find physically attractive. Being comfortable with your own sexuality. Staying in peak physical fitness and health. Capable of physically showing genuine emotions and feelings. (For example, *I eat only organic health food. I run five miles every weekday and spend an hour in the gym on Saturdays and Sundays. I do not smoke, drink alcohol, take illegal drugs, or abuse over-the-counter or prescription drugs. I take daily vitamins and supplements. I am capable and willing to use my body to fully interact with, and maintain a healthy balance within, my spirit, mind, and soul.*)

_____

_____

_____

_____

List three to five physical *weaknesses* or areas of improvement. These may include an imbalanced lifestyle where health is either overemphasized or downplayed. Getting sexually involved with someone outside of marriage. Being uncomfortable with your body or sexuality. Not accepting yourself as God created you. Having inaccurate perceptions or inappropriate inhibitions. (For example, *I do not like the overall shape of my body and wish God had created me differently. I am overly concerned about what others think of my appearance, and that causes me to have feelings of inadequacy. I have tried dieting and exercise, but they don't seem to help, so I tend to eat whatever I want whenever I want, which only makes things worse. I get involved physically outside of marriage as a way of receiving acceptance, affirmation, and affection even though I feel guilty and ashamed afterward.*)

_____

_____

_____

_____

_____

List three to five physical *requirements* you are looking for in a mate. These may include mutual attraction and chemistry. An appreciation for physical intimacy equal to your own. Maintaining a certain level of health and fitness. Having compatible sexual expectations and a desire to create and enjoy perpetual romance. (For example, *My ideal mate will love me for who I am and as God created me. She has a healthy confidence in her sexuality and demonstrates her affection for me by holding hands and kissing me, even in public. She uses terms of endearment for me that make me feel loved.*)

_____

_____

_____

_____

_____

Acknowledgement

As a new author, I've had a huge outpouring of encouragement, input, support, and prayers from quite a few people. It would be careless and thoughtless of me not to recognize those who have touched my life in so many amazing and unimaginable ways. My sincere and profound thanks to:

My kids – for still teaching me on a daily basis and for making me proud to be your dad. When you have kids of your own, you will understand.

Jack Dinsbeer – for your kind words and support in a difficult situation. Your gentle and humble spirit has been an inspiration to me for many years.

Gloria Gaither – for listening to the "still small voice" and reading through my initial manuscript. Your interest, encouragement, gentle persuasion, and guidance gave me hope when I needed it the most.

Kathy Ide – for your candid and challenging, yet professional, editing assistance. Your thought provoking comments gave a fresh perspective and made me dig a little deeper.

Mom and Dad Morrison – for making me a part of the family and for your enthusiasm, constant encouragement, and many prayers. Heaven only knows how things would have turned out without you in my life since high school.

Someone who prefers to be mentioned as Peter – the very fact you wish to remain anonymous while working zealously behind the scenes is evidence of your giving heart. Your generosity, encouragement (even if it was a well-deserved kick in the tail from time to time!), patience, challenging discussions, faithfulness, and friendship made this all possible. Only eternity will show the return on your investment.

Ernie Pinner – for your initial review and candid feedback of this work. Your professionalism, leadership, mentoring style, and friendship over the years are unmatched and invaluable to me. Thank you for taking a chance on a college kid many years ago.

Kris Swiatocho – for your special insight into the ministry of young adults and singles and your friendship, guidance, graphic artistry, speaking contacts, and all-around zaniness!

Jesus: my Savior, Lord, and soon-coming King – for your love, mercy, grace, forgiveness, and second chances. May you use this small offering of "loaves and fishes" to bless many others.

Endnotes

1   Martha Beck, "Lessons from 'Heartbreak Academy'" (from *O, the Oprah Magazine*, February 2003), http://www.cnn.com/2008/LIVING/personal/02/18/o.heartbreak.academy/index.html, accessed July 21, 2008.

2   *Children of Divorce Getting Divorced Themselves: Becoming Teen Moms, Single Moms, Battered Wives*, http://www.divorcereform.org/teenmoms.html, accessed July 20, 2008.

3   *Why Wait: The Benefits of Abstinence Until Marriage*, http://www.frc.org/get.cfm?i=IS06B01, accessed April 19, 2010.

4   Dr. James Dobson, *Why Are Some Men and Women Less Sensual than Others?*, http://family.custhelp.com/cgi-bin/family.cfg/php/enduser/std_adp.php?p_faqid=1068, accessed July 21, 2008.

5   Susan Graham Mathis, "Wanted: Marriage Veterans," *Focus on the Family* magazine, vol. 32, no. 2, 11-12, February 2008.

6   *Happily Never After: How Hollywood Favors Adultery and Promiscuity Over Marital Intimacy on Prime-Time Broadcast Television*, Parents Television Council study dated August 5, 2008, http://www.parentstv.org/PTC/news/release/2008/0805.asp, accessed August 11, 2008.

7   Ibid.

8   *U.S. Divorce Statistics*, http://www.divorcemag.com/statistics/statsUS.shtml, accessed July 20, 2008.

9   Ibid.

10 Hara Estroff Marano, *Divorced? Don't Even Think of Remarrying Until You Read This!* http://www.psychologytoday.com/articles/pto-20000301-000037.html, accessed August 23, 2008.

11 *U.S. Divorce Statistics,* http://www.divorcemag.com/statistics/statsUS.shtml, accessed July 20, 2008.

12 Ibid.

13 *U.S. Teenage Pregnancies, Births, and Abortions: National and State Trends and Trends by Race and Ethnicity,* http://www.guttmacher.org/pubs/USTPtrends.pdf, accessed February 8, 2010.

14 Ibid.

15 *U.S. Teen Sexual Activity,* http://www.kff.org/youthhivstds/upload/U-S-Teen-Sexual-Activity-Fact-Sheet.pdf, accessed July 19, 2008.

16 *U.S. Teenage Pregnancies, Births, and Abortions: National and State Trends and Trends by Race and Ethnicity,* http://www.guttmacher.org/pubs/USTPtrends.pdf, accessed February 8, 2010.

17 *Why Wait: The Benefits of Abstinence Until Marriage,* http://www.frc.org/get.cfm?i=IS06B01, accessed April 19, 2010.

18 *U.S. Teenage Pregnancies, Births, and Abortions: National and State Trends and Trends by Race and Ethnicity,* http://www.guttmacher.org/pubs/USTPtrends.pdf, accessed February 8, 2010.

19 *Module PD: Health and Well-Being (Parent Interview),* National Survey of Families and Households conducted by the University of Madison–Wisconsin, http://www.ssc.wisc.edu/nsfh/mod2/Phealth2.txt, accessed July 19, 2008.

20 *The Taxpayer Costs of Divorce: First Ever Estimates for the Nation and for all Fifty States,* http://center.americanvalues.org/?p=74, accessed July 20, 2008.

21 James Strong, *Strong's Exhaustive Concordance,* Hebrew and Chaldee Dictionary Accompanying the Exhaustive Concordance, word #430 (Crusade Bible Publishers, Inc., 1980), 12.

22 Wictionary, http://en.wiktionary.org/wiki/relativism, accessed January, 5, 2009.

23 Lee Strobel, *The Case for a Creator* (Grand Rapids, MI: Zondervan Publishing, 2004).

24 *Encarta World English Dictionary* (2009), http://uk.encarta. msn.com/encnet/features/dictionary/DictionaryResults.aspx ?lextype=3&search=interaction, accessed April 29, 2010.

25 Nate Stevens, *When Love Comes Calling*, composed May 1, 2008.

26 *Encarta World English Dictionary* (2009), http://uk.encarta.msn. com/encnet/features/dictionary/DictionaryResults.aspx?lexty pe=3&search=interdependence, accessed March 2, 2010.

27 Stephen R. Covey, *The Seven Habits of Highly Effective People* (Free Press, A Division of Simon & Schuster, Inc., 2004), 51.

28 *The Power of Connection: Physical, Emotional, and Spiritual Intimacy,* Mayo Clinic Health Solutions Special Report, October 2007, Mayo Foundation for Medical Education and Research.

29 Geert Hofstede, *Cultures and Organizations: Software of the Mind* (The McGraw-Hill Companies, Inc., 1997), 4, 238.

30 Spiros Zodhiates, Th.D., *The Hebrew-Greek Study Bible, King James Version,* Lexical Aids to the New Testament (AMG International, Inc. DBA AMG Publishers, 1991), 1750 (#4151).

31 James Strong, *Strong's Exhaustive Concordance,* Hebrew and Chaldee Dictionary Accompanying the Exhaustive Concordance, word #3820 (Crusade Bible Publishers, Inc., 1980), 58.

32 *Webster's New World College Dictionary,* http://www.your-dictionary.com/wisdom. accessed March 16 2010.

33 *Webster's New World College Dictionary,* http://www.your-dictionary.com/experience. accessed March 16, 2010.

34 Spiros Zodhiates, Th.D., *The Hebrew-Greek Study Bible, King James Version,* Lexical Aids to the New Testament (AMG International, Inc. DBA AMG Publishers, 1991), 1750 (#4151); 1769 (#5590).

35 Roger Fisher and Daniel I. Shapiro, *Beyond Reason: Using Emotions as You Negotiate* (Penguin Books, 2005), 11.

36 Billy Graham, *The Journey: How to Live by Faith in an Uncertain World* (Thomas Nelson Publishing, 2006), 177-178.

37 Phillip J. Swihart, "Did Barbie Change?" (excerpted from Focus on the Family's *Complete Guide to the First Five Years of Marriage,* Tyndale, 2006), http://www.family.org/marriage/A000001376.cfm, accessed August 2, 2008.

38   Max Lucado, *In The Eye of the Storm: A Day in the Life of Jesus* (Word Publishing, 1991), 240, 243.

39   Liane Yvkoff, *Sexual Incompatibility Troubles Marriages,* http://www.cnn.com/2008/LIVING/personal/03/03/sexless.marriage/index.html, accessed July 21, 2008.

40   Doug Houck, *Sexuality: Gift or Curse* (Metanoia Ministries), 1985, http://www.pureintimacy.org/gr/homosexuality/a0000073.cfm, accessed July 24, 2008.

41   George Barna, "Divorce Rates Among Religious Groups," http://www.religioustolerance.org/chr_dira.htm, accessed August 2, 2008.

42   Corinne McLaughlin and Davidson, Gordon, *The Deeper Side of Love and Relationship,* http://www.visionarylead.org/articles/love_relationship.htm, accessed July 21, 2008.

43   Elizabeth Cohen, *New Year's Resolution: Have More Sex,* http://www.cnn.com/2010/HEALTH/01/07/sex.health.benefits/index.html, accessed January 8, 2010.

44   *Why Wait: The Benefits of Abstinence Until Marriage,* http://www.frc.org/get.cfm?i=IS06B01, accessed April 19, 2010.

45   C. S. Lewis, *Mere Christianity* (HarperCollins Publishers, 1980), 116.

46   Sasha Emmons, *15 Everyday Romantic Gestures,* http://www.parenting.com/gallery/Mom/15-Everyday-Romantic-Gestures?hpt=Mid, accessed February 8, 2010.

47   Dr. Gary Chapman, *Five Love Languages: Learn the Languages,* http://www.5lovelanguages.com/learn-the-languages/the-five-love-languages, accessed April 6, 2010.

48   Daniel Todd Gilbert, *Stumbling on Happiness* (Alfred A. Knopf, a division of Random House, Inc., 2006), 183.

49   Rachel Fischer Spalding, *Do You Speak Body Language? The Signals You Send Trump What You Say,* December 20, 2008, http://www.lifescript.com/Life/Relationships/Also-in-relationships/Do_You_Speak_Body_Language.aspx, accessed April 13, 2010.

50   Celeste Perron, *Why You're Likely to Marry your Parent,* http://www.cnn.com/2009/LIVING/personal/02/11/lw.programmed.to.marry.parents/index.html, accessed February 15, 2009.

51   Stephanie Chen, *No Hooking Up: No Sex For Some Coeds,* http://

www.cnn.com/2010/LIVING/04/19/college.anti.hookup. culture/index.html?hpt=T2, accessed April 19, 2010.

52   Mission Statement, *Love & Fidelity Network*, http://loveand-fidelity.org/default.aspx?ID=7, accessed April 28, 2010.

53   Billy Graham, *The Journey: How to Live by Faith in an Uncertain World* (Thomas Nelson Publishing, 2006), 250.

54   *The Power of Connection: Physical, Emotional, and Spiritual Intimacy*, Mayo Clinic Health Solutions Special Report, October 2007 (Mayo Foundation for Medical Education and Research, 2007), 2.

55   Ibid, 1.

56   L. Coleen, *Emotional Intimacy*, http://www.selfgrowth.com/articles/ColeenL1.html, accessed August 15, 2008.

57   *The Power of Connection: Physical, Emotional, and Spiritual Intimacy*, Mayo Clinic Health Solutions Special Report, October 2007 (Mayo Foundation for Medical Education and Research, 2007), 5-6.

58   Dawn Eden, "The Significance of Sexual Intimacy" (excerpted from *The Thrill of the Chaste*, W Publishing Group, 2006), http://www.crosswalk.com/marriage/1442700, accessed July 24, 2008.

59   Dr. James Dobson, "Romance and Lifelong Intimacy" (adapted from Dr. James Dobson, *Five Essentials for Lifelong Intimacy*, Multnomah Publishers, Inc., 2005), http://www.family.org/marriage/A000001141.cfm?eafref=1, accessed July 21, 2008.

60   Dr. James Dobson, as quoted to him by his childhood Sunday school teacher, "What Factors Should I Consider Before Saying 'I do'?" http://family.custhelp.com/cgi-bin/family.cfg/php/enduser/std_adp.php?p_faqid=996, accessed July 29, 2008.

61   Spiros Zodhiates, Th.D., *The Hebrew-Greek Study Bible, King James Version*, Lexical Aids to the New Testament (AMG International, Inc. DBA AMG Publishers, 1991), 1644 (#5800).

62   *How Do You Balance Leave and Cleave with Honoring Your Parents?* http://www.gotquestions.org/leave-cleave-honor.html, accessed August 18, 2008.

63   C. S. Lewis, *Mere Christianity* (HarperCollins Publishers, 1980), 104.

64   James Strong, *Strong's Exhaustive Concordance*, Hebrew and Chal-

dee Dictionary Accompanying the Exhaustive Concordance, word #8055 (Crusade Bible Publishers, Inc., 1980), 118.

65   James Strong, *Strong's Exhaustive Concordance*, Greek Dictionary Accompanying the Exhaustive Concordance, word #700 (Crusade Bible Publishers, Inc., 1980), 15.

66   Maureen Salamon, *Housework and Sex: What's the Connection?* http://www.cnn.com/2008/LIVING/personal/06/17/housework.relationships, accessed July 28, 2008.

67   Lawrence Mark and Richard Sakai (producers), Cameron Crowe, (director), 1996, *Jerry McGuire*, USA, Sony/Columbia, http://www.boxofficemojo.com/movies/?id=jerrymaguire.htm, accessed April 26, 2010.

68   *Webster's New World College Dictionary*, http://www.yourdictionary.com/harsh, accessed March 16, 2010.

69   Stephen R. Covey, *The Seven Habits of Highly Effective People* (Published by Free Press, A Division of Simon & Schuster, Inc., 1989, 2004), 235.

70   James Strong, *Strong's Exhaustive Concordance*, Hebrew and Chaldee Dictionary Accompanying the Exhaustive Concordance, word #8055 (Crusade Bible Publishers, Inc., 1980), 118.

71   *Encarta World English Dictionary* (2009), http://uk.encarta. msn.com/encnet/features/dictionary/DictionaryResults. aspx?search=please&lextype=2, accessed April 27, 2010.

72   James Strong, *Strong's Exhaustive Concordance*, Greek Dictionary Accompanying the Exhaustive Concordance, word #700 (Copyright 1980, Crusade Bible Publishers, Inc), 15.

73   Ibid, word #7200, 106.

74   James Strong, *Strong's Exhaustive Concordance*, Greek Dictionary Accompanying the Exhaustive Concordance, words # 5362 and 5384 (Crusade Bible Publishers, Inc., 1980), 75 and 76.

75   Dr. Gary Chapman, *Five Love Languages: Learn the Languages*, http://www.5lovelanguages.com/learn-the-languages/the-five-love-languages, accessed April 6, 2010.

76   James Strong, *Strong's Exhaustive Concordance*, Greek Dictionary Accompanying the Exhaustive Concordance, word # 3366 (Crusade Bible Publishers, Inc., 1980), 51.

77   Proverb Quote, (n.d.), "Two heads are better than one,"

http://en.thinkexist.com/quotation/two_heads_are_better_than_one/196709.html, accessed April 26, 2010.

78 James Strong, *Strong's Exhaustive Concordance*, Greek Dictionary Accompanying the Exhaustive Concordance, word #4306 (Crusade Bible Publishers, Inc., 1980), 61.

79 Spiros Zodhiates, Th.D, *The Hebrew-Greek Study Bible, King James Version*, Lexical Aids to the New Testament, word #2428 (AMG International, Inc. DBA AMG Publishers, 1991), 1612.

80 *Webster's New World College Dictionary*, http://www.yourdictionary.com/virtue, accessed March 16, 2010.

81 *Encarta World English Dictionary* (2009), http://uk.encarta.msn.com/encnet/features/dictionary/DictionaryResults.aspx?search=virtuous&lextype=2, accessed April 26, 2010.

82 Matthew Henry, *Commentary on the Whole Bible*, vol. III, http://www.ccel.org/ccel/henry/mhc3.Prov.xxxii.html, accessed July 25, 2008.

83 James Strong, *Strong's Exhaustive Concordance*, Greek Dictionary Accompanying the Exhaustive Concordance, word #3860 (Crusade Bible Publishers, Inc., 1980), 61.

84 Spiros Zodhiates, Th.D, *The Hebrew-Greek Study Bible, King James Version*, Lexical Aids to the New Testament, word #25 (AMG International, Inc. DBA AMG Publishers, 1991), 1680.

85 Billy Graham, *The Journey: How to Live by Faith in an Uncertain World* (Thomas Nelson Publishing, 2006), p 247.

e|LIVE

---

listen|imagine|view|experience

AUDIO BOOK DOWNLOAD INCLUDED WITH THIS BOOK!

In your hands you hold a complete digital entertainment package. In addition to the paper version, you receive a free download of the audio version of this book. Simply use the code listed below when visiting our website. Once downloaded to your computer, you can listen to the book through your computer's speakers, burn it to an audio CD or save the file to your portable music device (such as Apple's popular iPod) and listen on the go!

How to get your free audio book digital download:

1. Visit www.tatepublishing.com and click on the e|LIVE logo on the home page.
2. Enter the following coupon code:
   0aca-94df-2d07-2295-ff32-3bd4-6575-a498
3. Download the audio book from your e|LIVE digital locker and begin enjoying your new digital entertainment package today!